HOPE ON THE BRINK
OF DESTRUCTION
A STUDY OF ISAIAH

STEVEN C. HUNTER

ISBN-10: 1941972845
ISBN-13: 978-1941972847

Published by Start2Finish Books
Fort Worth, Texas 76244
www.start2finish.org

Printed in the United States of America

Cover Design: Michael Whitworth

CONTENTS

1

THESE ARE TRYING TIMES

Isaiah is worthy to be said not only a prophet, but
more, a gospel, for he declares so openly…of Christ
and of [the] Holy Church, that you guess him not
only to ordain and profess a thing to come, but to
ordain a story of things passed.

Prologue to Isaiah in *The Wycliffe Bible*

We live each day faced with a barrage of sin. However, we have
no moral high ground to claim because we too have plenty of blame
to bear since we are fellow partakers in the sin plaguing the world.
God loves us despite our sin, and so we should also be able to give
that same God-like love to our neighbors. After all, we are told to
love our neighbors by Jesus, and he didn't mean for us to only love
those who were loveable. He also didn't attach any other qualifier on
his statement. God's love is perfect because it can love despite sin,
while our love is only easily given when it's not trampled.

The story of Isaiah is about God's love for His people. His nation. Many of His people acted and lived unworthily of His love — as we'd put it — but He loved them anyway. Isaiah is full of God's wrath, and I'd dare say that anytime something precious to any of us is threatened or mistreated, anger arises. God has always loved and demanded fidelity, and when his people refused to be faithful to Him, they provoked the anger and wrath of God. In the book of Isaiah, the Northern Kingdom of God's people is conquered and exiled by the Assyrians. God gave them over because they played the harlot with idols, among other things. Yet, God's undying love for His people led Him to promise that a remnant would return. Isaiah is primarily written to the Southern Kingdom of His people — Judah. Yet, there were also warnings and messages for the north and their conquerors.

It would be unrealistic to attempt to give an adequate verse-by-verse exposition of the book as a whole in thirteen lessons, so we won't try that here. Rather, we'll attempt to capture — with justice to this inspired prophecy — the overall mood of the book and God's message for His people of old. Isaiah is of particular interest, and rightly should be, to the Christian because it was quoted when Jesus revealed His person to the Jews in a synagogue after He'd been tempted in the wilderness (Luke 4:17–21). We see it also used to convert the Ethiopian Eunuch as he was on his way (Acts 8:27–35). As we come to the book of Revelation, we read about the cryptic seven spirits (Revelation 1:4; 5:6). A reading of Isaiah reveals seven particular characteristics of the Spirit that likely explain John's cryptic words (Isaiah 11:2).

Isaiah is the most frequently cited book in the New Testament. Portions of it that received the most attention were the voice in the desert (Isaiah 40:3), Immanuel's identity (Isaiah 7:14), Israel's disbelief and the remnant (Isaiah 1:9; 59:7–8), Jesus as the Prince of peace (Isaiah 9:2–7), and most popularly, the suffering servant (Isaiah 53). The Qumran community — among where the Dead Sea Scrolls were found — valued Isaiah as attested by the fragments of the book found there along with a commentary on Isaiah and numerous citations to Isaiah in other works. Therefore, if it were important to early Jews and the inspired New Testament writers, it should indeed — along with other facts mentioned — be read by Christians today.

ISAIAH: THE SETTING

Isaiah 1:1 gives us an idea of the time during which the prophet wrote. Four kings of Judah are named as those whose reign occupied the span of time during which the prophet ministered. Uzziah's reign began at 16 (2 Chronicles 26:1–3), and he reigned for 52 years (2 Kings 15:2), and did what was right in God's eyes. However, he didn't tear down the high places on which the people continually offered sacrifices (2 Kings 15:3–4). He became prideful later in his life and went in to burn incense on the altar of the Lord — a duty solely reserved for the priests. When the priests withstood him and he pressed his way in, God struck him with leprosy, and he was a leper the rest of his life (2 Chronicles 26:16–21). It was during the year that Uzziah died that Isaiah received his vision and call to the prophetic ministry (Isaiah 6:1ff).

Jotham's reign began at 25 years of age, and he reigned for 16 years (2 Kings 15:32–33). He followed his father's path of doing right but leaving the high places (2 Kings 15:34–35). Jotham's life is rather uneventful and pretty much follows that of his father's, but things would change with his son.

Ahaz's reign began when he was 20, and he reigned for 16 years (2 Kings 16:2). He, unlike his father and grandfather, walked in the ways of the kings of Israel — something we will learn was not good to do. He burned his children in sacrifice and acted as the nations the Lord drove out of the Promised Land. He also sacrificed on the high places and followed an idolatrous path (2 Kings 15:2–4). It was during Ahaz's reign that Israel was conquered by the Assyrians and exiled (2 Kings 17).

Hezekiah's reign began when he was 25, and he reigned for 29 years (2 Kings 18:2). It's said of him that "he did what was right in the eyes of the LORD, according to all that David his father had done" (2 Kings 18:3). One major theme in the books of the kings was whether a particular southern king (Judah) followed the ways of David. King David was the epitome of how a king should have conducted himself — David's own sins notwithstanding. David was the king with the heart after God. Even when King David failed, he'd be the first to repent when he became aware of his transgression, as was the case of his adultery with Bathsheba and the census. Hezekiah being paid this compliment is indicative of his striving to live righteously in service to God. He actually removed the high places and instituted many reforms that looked back to faithfulness, but they would not stand for his evil son, Manasseh's, reign. Most of the mentions of Isaiah outside the book that bears his name appear during Hezekiah's reign in the books of Kings and Chronicles.

ISAIAH: THE MAN

It's believed that Isaiah was born of an aristocratic family given the access he had to the king (Isaiah 7:3) and the familiarity he had with a priest (Isaiah 8:2). The early church scholar, Jerome (c. 347–420) likened him to Demosthenes, the orator, and poet, for the beauty of his writing. Since he began his ministry in the year Uzziah died (Isaiah 6:1), scholars place the dating of his ministry from 739–686 B.C. (52 years). His ministry as a whole would consist of him warning and exhorting people who simply wouldn't listen (Isaiah 6:9–13) — a feeling many preachers can identify with. A study of the Old

Testament places Isaiah as a contemporary of Hosea and Micah.

Isaiah prophesied primarily to a divided kingdom and foretold of Jerusalem's impending fall to the Babylonians. He identified the empty worship of God's people by their failure to live righteously (Isaiah 1:10–15) as well as their idolatrous behavior (Isaiah 40:18–20). We know that he lived at least until 681 B.C. when he penned an account of the Assyrian king Sennacherib's death (cf. Isaiah 37:38). Tradition has it that Isaiah died during the reign of Manasseh, Hezekiah's son. He died, tradition tells us, by being cut in two with a wooden saw. Several believe that Hebrews 11:37 was a reference to Isaiah, among others.

ISAIAH: THE BOOK

The book may be divided as follows:

- **Chapters 1–5:** Isaiah describes the Lord's complaints against Judah and Israel, the future glory of Zion and the coming day of the Lord.

- **Chapters 6–8:** God calls Isaiah and commissions him for ministry.

- **Chapters 9–12:** God will use the nations to punish the Israelites, who will ultimately be destroyed by the Assyrians; however, a remnant will return to the land and the Assyrians will be destroyed.

- **Chapters 13–23:** Isaiah prophesies judgments against surrounding nations.

- **Chapters 24–27:** Isaiah predicts universal judgment and God's ultimate triumph over evil.

- **Chapters 28–35:** Isaiah prophesies against Ephraim, Jerusalem, Lebanon and the Assyrians; God speaks of the Messiah's ministry, the day of the Lord and Israel's restoration and glory in the kingdom.

- **Chapters 36–39:** Isaiah describes the siege of Jerusalem; God extends Hezekiah's life; Babylonian exile is predicted.

- **Chapters 40–48:** Isaiah speaks of God's comfort of His people after judgment, assuring them that God will deliver them.

- **Chapters 49–57:** Isaiah prophesies about the Messiah's obedience, mission, suffering, and crucifixion; God promises the Israelites that He still loves them in spite of their sin and has not forsaken them.

- **Chapters 58–66:** Isaiah describes Israel's sins, the consequences and the need for repentance; he reveals God's future involvement with the Gentile nations and with Israel.[1]

ISAIAH: THE LESSONS

I believe one good place to start is with the first two kings mentioned — Uzziah and Jotham. Both are recorded as having been good kings, but the stipulation is added that they left the high places. When we become comfortable surrounded by ungodliness, we are only a generation away from someone who'll embrace it. Ahaz came along, and because his daddy and granddaddy left those high places, he must have seen them and believed that if they were there then they weren't as bad as some of the righteous made them out to be. They had been "tolerated" previously, so why not "use" them now? We must remember what Paul said, "A little leaven leavens the whole lump" (1 Corinthians 5:6). An example of how this might translate into our modern lives is this: some of us may have that bottle of liquor in the cabinet at home. A few generations ago our good, godly ancestors kept it because they used it for medicine. How long before a generation arises that uses it simply for socialization? Sure, it may not be harming anyone in that cabinet. It may indeed not be hurting us personally, but someone else comes along and sips and finds that they like the taste. Before long it's all that they can crave. Not long after that, it's all that they want. The leaven ruined the dough. You can insert anything into this. I think something more relevant to faithful Christians is apathy, myself. No one else is doing XYZ, so I'll not do it either. How many of us are surrounded by dying congregations held together by a few old folks? In the South, it's a sad epidemic. Those congregations are facing these struggles because they quit preaching the good news to lost souls due to laziness and apathy. Maybe there was a split, but congregations can rebuild after a split if they focus on preaching the good news of Jesus. What are the high places in your life that need to be purged? Find them and purge them now, because you don't want to leave them for those who come after you to cozy up to.

Ahaz was the king who cozied up to the high places. But his unrighteous actions went even deeper as he began acting like those who made the high places a focal point of their mode of operation. The nation descended into further sin because her leader led her there. However, repeatedly in Isaiah, the prophet reminded the reader that a remnant would return and be faithful. In the midst of sin and human vice, there are always those faithful souls — no matter how few they may be — who stand firmly with and for God. In the account of Sodom and Gomorrah, we see the righteousness of Lot (cf. 2 Peter 2:7). Alas, righteous Lot was grossly outnumbered, and the cry of that wicked city came up to God's ears (Genesis 18:20ff). There comes a point at which God's righteousness must meet the evils of His own creation. Judgment is the only option left when God has done everything to urge His people to repent and they fail to do just that.

As we look around at the United States of America, we see a country once given to God now departing swiftly from Him. Perhaps it's us who love Him and endeavor to serve Him that stays His hand of judgment on our land. Then again, maybe our nation is in need of His judgment. Yet, there may be a leader somewhere on the horizon, a voice of reason and righteousness that will arise and stand more for God than an ideal that goes against Him. From an earthly standpoint, Hezekiah was Isaiah's hope, but God was the prophet's ultimate hope. When he was surrounded by every reason to despair, he pressed on. When God charged that his ministry be one of preaching that would not be heeded, the prophet still said, "Here am I, send me!"

FILL IN THE BLANK

1. Anger is motivated first by _____.

2. The Northern Kingdom fell during _____ reign.

3. Which of the four kings during which Isaiah prophesied was the most righteous — likened to King David? _____

4. Isaiah was a contemporary of _____ and _____.

5. He penned an account of the _____ king _____'s death which leads us to believe that he lived until 681 B.C.

DISCUSSION QUESTIONS

1. What was the particular passage from which the Ethiopian Eunuch read in Acts 8:27–35 and how did (does) it explain Jesus?

   Isaiah 53:78

2. If Isaiah was so valuable to early Christianity, why does it seem all but obsolete in the mind of Christians today? Does modern Christianity give proper attention to the Old Testament as a whole?

3. After reading Isaiah 6:9–13 and seeing the type of response Isaiah would receive, how challenging do you think the work of a preacher is? What can we do to help preachers in their work?

NOTES

1. http://www.bibleversesabout.org/bible/isa/.

2

THE HOLY ONE OF ISRAEL

As [man] tried, disobeying, to mount high,
    and so he is shut out, for just this cause,
    from making satisfaction for himself.
It had to be by God's own ways, God's laws,
    that to his true life man might be restored:
    I mean by both God's pardon and the Cross.

Dante, *Paradiso*

One December not too long ago, my wife and I had a date night. We went to Nashville, TN from Bowling Green, KY to attend a performance of Handel's *Messiah* at the Schermerhorn Symphony Center. *Messiah* is the famous oratorio composed in the eighteenth century that is entirely about Jesus and the Gospel. It's usually played near Christmas for obvious reasons. As we sat in our seats, I kept hearing, in the lyrics, Messianic passages from the book of Isaiah. I heard the chorus sing about His virgin birth and suffering among the many other passages that depicted Jesus. It was absolutely beautiful.

When the conductor led the orchestra to the "Hallelujah Chorus" — the most famous part of this entire piece — I was so amazed by what happened next. Once the introductory notes to this piece were played, everyone in the symphony hall rose to their feet. It gave me chills. Here I was in a symphony hall where people were standing as this was sung to God. Mind you, artsy folks tend not to be so religious. Nevertheless, this beautiful music led us all to stand to our feet as if we were in the very presence of God.

The hit song that was on Christian radio years ago, *I Can Only Imagine*, is another song whose lyrics make you wonder. When the artist sings, "Will I stand in Your presence? Or to my knees will I fall? … I can only imagine," I can't help but wonder what that day will be like when we stand before our Creator…our God…our Savior.

One of the most tragic offenses of humanity is our loss of the wonder of God Almighty. We no longer tremble at the thought of His awesome power. Part of the reason, I might suggest, is that we're too intellectual. Because we understand things so clearly, we lose the thrill of joy and the beauty of our amazement at them. Think about how joyful a child is over a blossoming flower, or the snow when it falls on the ground. They look at the beauty of God's creation and are utterly amazed while we often snub our noses at such things in nature because our faces are buried in tablets and smartphones.

Jesus said that we must become like little children to inherit the kingdom of heaven (Matthew 18:3). When I think about a child, I consider many traits that we adults lose as we become numb to the world. Wonder is one. I'd dare bet, if I were a gambling man, that a child would recognize Jesus today if He walked the earth. However, I doubt many of us adults would know Him at all if He walked the earth today. We accept things as they are when we grow up, and we don't usually reserve joy for such things as God's creation. Our hearts are like huge calluses because we've become too accustomed to the harshness of the world. When we lose the wonder of God Almighty, we become as Israel was — idolatrous. We are driven by covetousness, evil desires, and our passions which Paul said were idolatrous (Colossians 3:5).

THE GOD WHO IS HOLY

In Isaiah, God is depicted as "holy." The Hebrew term translated as "holy" (*qadosh*) appears over thirty times throughout the entire book. It's only used once of God's people, and the rest of the time it's used of God. He's often called "the Holy One of Israel" in Isaiah. Given that Israel was accustomed to the multiplicity of pagan idols (Isaiah 44:6–11; 46:1–2, 5–7; 57:3–10), God being "One" was significant. God entreated Israel to regard Him as "holy" — "But the LORD of hosts, him you shall honor as holy. Let him be your fear, and let him be your dread" (Isaiah 8:13). Acknowledging God as holy was something that Israel failed to do.

The prophet shares his call to ministry by the vision he saw. In the year that King Uzziah died, Isaiah writes,

> I saw the Lord sitting upon a throne, high and lifted up; and the train of his robe filled the temple. Above him stood the seraphim. Each had six wings: with two he covered his face, and with two he covered his feet, and with two he flew. And one called to another and said: "Holy, holy, holy is the LORD of hosts; the whole earth is full of his glory!" And the foundations of the thresholds shook at the voice of him who called, and the house was filled with smoke. And I said: "Woe is me! For I am lost; for I am a man of unclean lips, and I dwell in the midst of a people of unclean lips; for my eyes have seen the King, the LORD of hosts!" Then

one of the seraphim flew to me, having in his hand a burning coal that he had taken with tongs from the altar. And he touched my mouth and said: "Behold, this has touched your lips; your guilt is taken away, and your sin atoned for." (Isaiah 6:1–7)

Two things stick out to me from this passage: at the proclamation of God's holiness, the foundations of the thresholds shook. What does it say when even created elements that lack life know to tremble at the voice of Him who calls? Second, Isaiah was immediately reminded of his sinfulness. He cried out a "woe" upon himself because his own nakedness was bare in the presence of the Holy God.

Isaiah's vision in the throne room of God is the most striking depiction of God throughout the entire book, in my opinion. I nearly feel as if I should kneel at a reading of this passage. The fiery Angels, Seraphim, stood as "bodyguards, as it were, like a crown from all sides" (Eusebius *Comm. Isaiah* 6.2). According to John Chrysostom (c. 349–407), he believed that the Seraphim protected God's image since God dwelt in unapproachable light (cf. 1 Timothy 6:16).

Moses had once requested to see God's glory, but God replied that no man could see His face and live (Exodus 33:18–20). When Nadab and Abihu offered profane fire to God, He struck them dead and then told Aaron that He was to be regarded as holy by those who drew near to Him (Leviticus 10:1–3). Even later, Uzzah touched the Ark of the Covenant and God struck Him dead since only a particular family of the Levites were permitted to transport the ark (2 Samuel 6:1–9). In each of these stories, God acted in ways to preserve His holiness. How awesome and reverend is our God! We should be reminded never to regard any exercise of devotion or worship flippantly. Let us avoid such dishonor by reflecting upon God's holiness beforehand.

THE SPLENDOR OF HIS MAJESTY

Three times in Isaiah 2, we read of the splendor of God's majesty (vv. 10, 19, 21). Don Shackleford wrote that the particular phrase stressed "the uniqueness of God in judgment and worship."[1] On the front end of Isaiah's prophecy, this notion of God's majesty stood forth in contrast to the idols Israel worshipped. Those gods were fashioned from metal and wood. Man bowed down and worshipped them, but God alone was worthy of worship. The people cried to the idols for their wants and needs, but only God was fair in giving what should have been given. The remaining remnant of God's people who'd survive conquering and exile would sing over the "majesty" of the Lord (Isaiah 24:14). This term is even used of Jesus — God's Branch (Isaiah 4:2; cf. Isaiah 11:1–5; 2 Corinthians 4:5; 2 Peter 1:16).

THE GOD WHO SERVES

In an unusual turn of events, the God who had been discarded by Israel is depicted as Holy and Majestic, but He eventually condescends to the status of a suffering servant:

> He was despised and rejected by men; a man of sorrows, and acquainted with grief; and as one from whom men hide their faces he was despised, and we esteemed him not. (Isaiah 53:3)

God had chosen Israel as His servant (41:8; 44:1–2). However, as God had told Isaiah about his preaching, Israel became deaf and blind (42:19). Popular opinion became more important to them than God's opinion (Isaiah 2:22). They no longer depended on God alone. They turned to the vast sin of self-reliance (Isaiah 22:8–11; cf. Deut.

8:17–20). Perhaps since they didn't want a majestic and holy King, they would turn their attention to a servant. In contrast to Israel's failed service to God, the Servant of the Lord (Acts 3:13) would fulfill all the work that God gave Him (Luke 13:32; John 17:4). These servant passages are:

- Isaiah 42:1–9 (cf. Matthew 12:18–20)
- Isaiah 49:1–13
- Isaiah 50:4–11
- Isaiah 52:13–53:12

THE LESSONS

When we consider and reflect upon our God's holiness and majesty, it should give us a moment of pause. In Exodus 19, God had told Moses to prepare the people for the third day for when He would descend on Sinai. They were given three days to prepare to appear before God's presence. What does it say when we constantly run late on Sunday morning to worship? Let alone, what does it say when we peruse Facebook during worship or clip our fingernails? I think it says that we don't take the holiness and majesty of our God seriously. I'm struck with amusement when people act so on-point before an earthly dignitary such as Queen Elizabeth II or the Pope. We see all the pomp and circumstance with them, so people behave reverently. Just because we cannot see God before us doesn't give us a pass to act haphazardly.

In our sinfulness, God would be justified to pour out His divine wrath upon us all. However, He chose to take the form of a servant, gird Himself with a towel, and wash His disciples' feet. In all of the religions of the world, God is the only one — as far as I know — who loves His creation so much that He'd become exactly what we are so that we could become what He is: "For our sake he made him to be sin who knew no sin, so that in him we might become the righteousness of God" (2 Corinthians 5:21). Another passage Paul used read, "For you know the grace of our Lord Jesus Christ, that though he was rich, yet for our sake he became poor, so that you by his poverty might become rich" (2 Corinthians 8:9).

What lessons can we learn? When we consider what God became for us, we should be more giving of our mercy to others who sin against us. Also, when we consider what we actually deserve from God, we should bow in humility before Him and be gracious to others. We have not been given what we deserve. We've been given grace. Let's learn to forgive as God forgives. Let's learn not to hop on our high-horse of judgment, but let's condescend with a towel around our waist, with a basin of water, prepared to wash the dirt of others.

FILL IN THE BLANK

1. God is often referred to as _____ in Isaiah.

2. Man cannot see God's _____ and live.

3. In Isaiah 2, we read about the splendor of God's _____.

4. Who is God's Branch? _____

5. Jesus was made to know _____ so that we can know the _____ of God.

DISCUSSION QUESTIONS

1. Given Paul's understanding of idolatry in Colossians 3:5, what types of idolatry do we face today?

2. What are ways that we can regard God as holy compared to what we do?

3. How is self-reliance a sin?

4. How does viewing our holy and majestic God as a servant impact the way we should view others?

NOTES

1. Don Shackleford, *Isaiah: Truth For Today Commentary* (Searcy: Resource Publications, 2005), 58.

3

THE PRIDE OF SIN

Righteousness exalts a nation, but sin is a reproach to any people.

Proverbs 14:34

At the beginning of God's accusations against Israel, God noted that their sins were as scarlet (Isaiah 1:18). The notion of scarlet sins carried the idea of Israel having such a habitual inclination to sin that it would seem as if their guilt would be incapable of cleansing. Yet, in that same verse, God promised that though their sins were as scarlet, they should be as white as snow. However, before they could be as white as snow, Israel had to face the music of their own sinfulness.

When sin is a problem, the best thing to do is to confront it head on. We should never bury our head in the sand; rather we need to face what God's Word says about sin and let Him inform us. The problem too many have today is that they place their trust in themselves and say, "I'm a good person." This is rather arrogant given that even Jesus refused to be called "good" (Luke 18:18–19). If we were actually good, He wouldn't have had to face the cross, so we need to be realistic about our own sinfulness and what God requires of us.

CELEBRATING SIN PUBLICLY

When we speak about Israel's sins, we're talking about actions that are clearly and directly opposed to God's Word, not actions that might depend on motivation or understanding or other factors that could cause ambiguity in determining if they are sinful. At the first congregation where I preached, an elderly lady once asked me if it were sinful to play cards. I played Uno and Old Maid as well as other card games, so I asked what she meant. She told me that she was brought up to believe that card-playing was sinful in itself. Given her age, gambling was associated with card playing, so her parents taught her to think that card playing was wicked. Now, you and I know that playing a card game isn't inherently immoral, but some Christians believe that individual acts like these are inherently sinful. When we speak about Israel's sins, we're talking about matters of opinion. We'll be discussing explicit wrongdoings according to God.

When people cozy up to sin, it usually follows a progression. In Psalm 1:1, the sinner begins by walking, then standing, and finally sitting. Each sequence leads to a greater level of comfort with sin. When people lose their moral bearings and give in to sin, they eventually see it as nothing wrong and run headlong into sin so much so that it is no longer hidden.

> For the look on their faces bears witness against them; they proclaim their sin like Sodom; they do not hide it. Woe to them! For they have brought evil on themselves. (Isaiah 3:9)

Would God have us to believe that He'd prefer that we sin privately? No! When sin is celebrated openly, it is because the holiness of God has been ignored and humanity has established their own righteousness that is not God's righteousness (cf. Romans 10:1–3). The Lord's righteousness will never be dismayed (Isaiah 51:6) because it is eternal (Isaiah 51:8). Israel's self-righteous idolatry was false because it was intermingled with the pure religion of God (cf. Isaiah 57:12). They wanted to include their idolatry with the pure worship of God and call it "righteous." They had underestimated the ways of God (Isaiah 55:8–9) so that even their thoughts were sinful (Isaiah 59:7).

The one who does righteousness is the one who remembers God and His ways (Isaiah 64:5; cf. 32:17). The one who does his own righteousness — without being mindful of God's righteousness — presents themselves to God as unclean, filthy rags (Isaiah 64:6). The imagery of the polluted garment references the stained menstrual garment of a woman (cf. Leviticus 15:19–31). God couldn't have used any stronger image than that of the polluted garment. Therefore, when we take it upon ourselves to set up our own righteousness without being mindful of God's righteousness, we present soiled garments that do not lead to salvation.

CALLING SIN "GOOD"

If we become comfortable with sin, it begins to take on a whole new shape before too long. No longer do we think of it as "sin," but as "good." Don't we see a lot of things in our own country right now called "good" that simply aren't?

> Woe to those who call evil good and good evil, who put darkness for light and light for darkness, who put bitter for sweet and sweet for bitter! (Isaiah 5:20)

Publicly celebrated sin is sometimes called "progress." Sometimes it's thought to be enlightenment. At other times, it's a "choice" or "disease". Phyllis McGinley (1905–78) wrote an essay entitled "The Consolations of Illiteracy." In her essay, she commented on sin by writing, "Sin has always been an ugly word, but it has been made so with a new sense over the past half-century. It has been one not only ugly by passe. People are no longer sinful; they are only immature, or underprivileged, or frightened, or, more particularly, sick." Commenting on this passage from her essay, a Jesuit priest, James V. Schall, wrote, "Sin includes will and such words as 'sick' or 'immature' are usually employed to prevent us from seeing that sin cannot fully be explained by anything else *but* will."[1]

At least in this context, God identifies a part of the problem as being a lack of knowledge (Isaiah 5:13). Israel failed to know God (Isaiah 1:3). Furthermore, because they lacked knowledge, they couldn't discern between what was good and bad (Isaiah 27:11). One would like to believe that ignorance is a good enough excuse not to be held accountable to God. However, when you're expected to know, you'd best search for the truth or else face the consequences (Isaiah 42:22–25). To not seek to know is equivocated with a rejection of real knowledge by God (Isaiah 5:24). If a person believes that he is wise (Isaiah 5:21; cf. 32:5–8), he doesn't see the need to search for heavenly truths. This kind of self-sufficiency goes so far as to lead to poor governing of a people (Isaiah 10:1). It was a staple of Babylon (Isaiah 47:10).

REJECTING HEAVENLY REVELATION

When Israel believed themselves to be wise in their own eyes, they no longer wanted divine revelation. In Isaiah 8:16, the prophet requested that his prophecy be sealed up. This was to protect the message from those who might tamper with it, and it was also for posterity. In Isaiah 30:8, he was to record the entire message to serve as a record for God's people — akin to what was written in 8:16 and also in 34:16. The people wanted to hear pleasant words, not words of warning. They instructed the prophets to remain silent and prohibited the seers from telling their visions (Isaiah 30:10). Yet, God's Word would prevail (Isaiah 40:6–8). God wished that His commandments would have prevailed in the lives of His people, but they hadn't (Isaiah 48:18–19). The going out of His Word through the prophet would have an influence (Isaiah 55:11), but sadly that influence would not be immediate.

By the time of God's judgment, His sinning people would realize the futility of their own wisdom and knowledge in comparison to God's. They would be left no longer prideful, but fearful (Isaiah 33:14), because they had burdened God with their sins (Isaiah 43:24). Had they actually wanted to be righteous, they would have listened to the prophet and His divine revelation. As it was, they didn't want anything to do with him or the message he brought because it didn't make them feel good.

THE LESSONS

For Christians who seek to live lives pleasing to God, it is necessary for us to approach this particular lesson with great humility. It can be tempting to point out Israel's faults while being complacent to the fact that we too are not without error. Looking at the sins of others can tempt us to judge them while offering our "amens" to the preacher who denounces these things, but we must be careful not to fall into the error of puffing ourselves up while looking down on Israel.

We all probably know people who have lived lives of scarlet sinfulness — they seemed unrepentant and even rejoiced in some measure over their sin(s). We have a responsibility as those who may be spiritually minded to love our neighbor enough to warn them (Galatians 6:1–2; cf. James 5:19–21). While doing this, we're to regard them as brethren and not enemies (2 Thessalonians 3:15), which may be a temptation when dealing with a scarlet sinner. In Matthew 18:15–17, Jesus gave a threefold process of how to address such a person.

When working with someone who's in sin, the temptation exists to do nothing. Why? One reason is because those who would deal with a sinner are not without sin themselves. Moreover, the guilty party might retort, "Who are you to judge me?" There may be other reasons why we'd prefer silence over the noise of confrontation. Isaiah pointed out his own sin before God, but that didn't eliminate him from preaching God's word to the people. Was Isaiah a person who sinned? Yes. However, he was not a scarlet sinner who lived unrepentant to God. There's a difference between a person who lives a life of scarlet sinfulness versus a person who sins but tries to follow God. However, the argument that no one should become involved is as unloving as if God sat on the sidelines while we fell to our own sinfulness. Also, anyone who'd suggest "minding their own business" has apparently not read or are altogether unfamiliar with the very notion of a prophet.

Another lesson to learn here is that human intelligence certainly has its limitations. The mind cannot conceive of everything. This is why divine revelation exists — it fills in what the mind cannot grasp. Schall writes in another book of his, *On the Unseriousness of Human Affairs,*

> Were reason able to arrive at the knowledge of the highest things [divine knowledge] by its own powers alone, we would already be gods. We would not need anything more than our own intelligences to know

all that is; however, this seems obviously not to be the case. Likewise, it is "heretical" to maintain that there are "two truths," one from reason and one from revelation, which can contradict each other yet both be "true." Revelation and reason belong to the same universe. We cannot have it otherwise.[2]

God plainly told His people that the secret things belonged to Him, but those things that were revealed were given so that His people could obey His commandments (Deuteronomy 29:29). This prophecy of Isaiah was published for their benefit (cf. Isaiah 8:20), as the entire Bible exists for our benefit.

FILL IN THE BLANK

1. The imagery of Israel's sins being as scarlet communicated that they were _____ sinners incapable of being _____.

2. According to Psalm 1:1, the progression of sin begins by _____, is followed by standing, and culminates with _____.

3. A part of Israel's problem was a lack of _____ of God.

4. They wanted positive _____ and not a message of warning.

5. When people are scarlet sinners, we have a responsibility to warn them. We shouldn't use excuses because _____ confessed his sin at the beginning of this book.

DISCUSSION QUESTIONS

1. What's the problem with this statement, "I'm a good person?"

2. Discuss sins that are celebrated publicly. Since sins are often called by different names other than sin, what name do these publicly-celebrated sins go by?

3. What do some people call "sinful" today that the Bible may not actually identify as sinful?

4. What's the best way to carry out what Jesus urges in Matthew 18:15–17?

NOTES

1. James V. Schall, *The Life of the Mind: On the Joys and Travails of Thinking* (Wilmington, ISI Books, 2006), 67.

2. James V. Schall, *On the Unseriousness of Human Affairs* (Wilmington: ISI Books, 2012), 113.

4

FAILED LEADERSHIP

That I had someone—as a ruler and as a father—who could keep me from being arrogant and make me realize that even at court you can live without a troop of bodyguards, and gorgeous clothes, lamps, sculpture—the whole charade. That you can behave almost like an ordinary person without seeming slovenly or careless as a ruler or when carrying out official obligations.

Marcus Aurelius *Meditations*

I used to work for a man who was a multi-millionaire. He was an older man who had worked in several industries as an entrepreneur. He'd failed, and he'd succeeded. His latest success was during the era of pagers (for those who remember what a pager was). He owned a company that produced pagers and took it public for a $200 million merger, and he made a boatload not long before the pager industry tanked. He knew when to get out.

During the time I worked for his company, I was able to spend time with him. He'd come into town, usually for a day or two every month or so to market and try to grow the business. His life was consumed with work. The lessons that I gleaned from him have served me well and have proven useful even as a minister. Earthly success is nothing bad. However, how we view it can be bad. We can be greedy and ungracious, or we can handle the success in a Christian way. I'm convinced that not everyone is fit to handle success like this man had, and that's not to say that he handled it well.

I enjoyed working for him because as someone who was successful in an earthly measure, he thought differently from most people. It was always the little things. In conversation I once stated, "I don't care," only as a joke. However, he saw an opportunity to teach me a lesson. He told me that I should always care, and that nothing, not even the smallest detail, should escape my attention. I've reflected on that advice, and he was right.

At times, we'd lose a little money here or there in managing the business. In light of the greater picture, it wasn't too much when you consider the yearly income. However, to this man, every penny mattered. I heard an employee say something like, "It was only a couple of dollars." The owner went into a tirade about how pitiful that attitude was.

I say all of this only to point out that this man was a genuine leader. He was good at it. He made you want to listen to him no matter how farfetched his words were. He'd succeeded in life, in an earthly way. In that same advice I saw spiritual connections. I thought, "What if we viewed our Christianity the same way we viewed this business?" The truth is that striving for excellence, when given the proper Christian perspective, is actually glorifying God.

Israel, however, was a different story. They lacked leadership. They lacked someone to rush into tirades about doing right…about giving your best. Because of failed leadership, among many other problems, they were facing the wrath of God.

We mustn't ever underestimate the value of good or poor leadership. It has an influence, and that influence can determine the success or downfall of a people.

ISRAEL'S LEADERSHIP ISSUE

By the time of Isaiah, Israel had long been a monarchy. Before that time, the nation was ruled by judges. The judges and priests had similar legal authority according to Moses Law (Deut. 17:8–13), but the king was to have had absolute authority in matters of state. The Levites and priests were to ensure that the king had a copy of Moses' Law for his personal use (Deut. 17:18–20). It's clear that this wasn't a reality with Israel's kings. While it isn't explicitly mentioned throughout the Bible, we may infer that at least David might have had access to the written Law. When he and others transported the Ark to Jerusalem, it was transported on an ox-cart. The outcome was the loss of Uzzah's life. Later when they finally were able to transport the ark, David is recorded as saying that only the Levites were able to transport it since they were authorized to handle it. We may infer that he'd searched the Law to see how the Ark was to be transported.

However, in Isaiah's time, no leader in any position — king, priests, judges, elders — did what was pleasing to God. The result was an absence of leadership during the siege of Jerusalem (Isaiah 3:2–3). Only nine of the leaders listed there were legitimate while the others were not (diviner and enchanter). This tragedy resulted in the infidelity of God's people. When reading Isaiah, we must keep in mind that the whole nation was wicked and idolatrous. We must also remember that the nation had leaders whose job was to instruct the people in God's ways and carry out the necessary discipline when they erred. Any time people are immoral, one need only to look to their leaders.

So the LORD cut off from Israel head and tail, palm branch and reed in one day—the elder and honored man is the head, and the prophet who teaches lies is the tail; for those who guide this people have been leading them astray, and those who are guided by them are swallowed up. (Isaiah 9:14–17)

This prophecy may have referred to the destruction of Samaria in 722 B.C. or the chaos that ensued after Jeroboam II. During the latter of these two, the people had no leadership.

REMOVED FROM POWER

Shebna was the head of Hezekiah's household — a prominent position in itself (2 Kings 18:18). He was in an envoy who negotiated with the Assyrian general (2 Kings 18:18–37). When the description of him is read as a continuation of the prophecy about Jerusalem, Shebna personified the apathy of Israel. Shebna is meant to represent someone who was very earthly minded. He cared more for the comforts and accolades of here than pleasing God. Therefore, God would replace him with Eliakim, who would be faithful to the Lord and King (Isaiah 22:20–25). Shebna was demoted, as the prophecy states, and we see him later referred to as a "secretary" (2 Kings 18:37; Isaiah 36:3).

An apparent change of behavior followed this change in Hezekiah's house. Eliakim returns to Hezekiah in grief after hearing how Judah would suffer at the hands of the Assyrians (Isaiah 36:22). Other counselors might have brushed off the report, or sought the ear-tickling of their household prophets. Eliakim even led the household to adorn themselves with the proper garments of mourning. Then, instead of going to those treacherous false prophets, he led, at Hezekiah's command, the household of the king to Isaiah concerning their report (Isaiah 37:2). In the next lesson, we will consider more closely how Israel trusted more in instruments of warfare than God before this change in the king's household.

THE GOOD SHEPHERD

From chapter 40 onward Isaiah adopts a change in tone. He's looking to the end of the Babylonian captivity. Messianic passages become more prominent from this point toward the end of the book. Of the passages of Isaiah quoted in the New Testament, fifty verses derive from chapters 40–66, and many of them refer directly to the Messiah (Jesus). It would only stand to reason that this passage below is read with the Messiah in mind.

> Behold, the Lord GOD comes with might, and his arm rules for him; behold, his reward is with him, and his recompense before him. He will tend his flock like a shepherd; he will gather the lambs in his arms; he will carry them in his bosom, and gently lead those that are with young. (Isaiah 40:10–11)

It brought to mind the words of Christ—

> I am the good shepherd. The good shepherd lays down his life for the sheep. He who is a hired hand and not a shepherd, who does not own the sheep, sees the wolf coming and leaves the sheep and flees, and the wolf snatches them and scatters them. He flees because he is a hired hand and cares nothing for the sheep. I am the good shepherd. I know my own and

my own know me. (John 10:11–14)

THE LESSONS

When it comes to spiritual leadership, I believe this is a great lesson to learn from. We who engage in shepherding the Lord's people have a responsibility not only to them, but to Him. While I'm only a preacher, let's speak to the reality of the church today—the preacher does more leading, often times, than the shepherds of congregations. Many of the pastoral responsibilities of congregations are bestowed, officially or unofficially, on the preachers. People will often look to them before going to their elders. It's a rare congregation that the Christians go to their shepherds before their preacher. Let's be sure that we as preachers point fellow Christians in the right direction. It's not merely enough to teach what the Scriptures teach if we fail to do it. Many congregations teach and preach that the elders are the pastors of the church, but in practice, this is far from the truth for many.

Furthermore, elders should be better educated in matters of faith than the preacher(s). Most elders are biblically literate, but preachers undergo specialized training to be proclaimers of God's Word. While elders may not have the opportunity for specialized training, they should be men who constantly seek growth and desire to learn what the Scriptures teach on a deeper level. I once spoke with a preacher at a church who lamented the doctrinal division among his elders. Part of the problem could have been some of their understanding of the Scriptures. A greater source of the problem had to do with pride. Regardless, shepherds should know as much if not more of God's Word than preachers.

FILL IN THE BLANK

1. Before Israel was ruled by a monarch, they were ruled by
_____.

2. Of the leaders mentioned in Isaiah 2, the
_____ and _____ were not
legitimate leaders according to Moses' Law.

3. _____ replaced _____ as the
head of Hezekiah's household.

4. From Isaiah chapter _____ onward, Isaiah adopted a
change in tone.

5. _____ verses derive from Isaiah chapters 40–66.

DISCUSSION QUESTIONS

1. What's the importance of good leadership?

2. Is leadership always to blame for a failed group of people?
Why or why not? Consider this: since Adam and Eve sinned,
did God fail as a leader?

3. How and why is the position of the preacher in the local
church sometimes treated unscripturally?

5

THE WAY OF CAIN

That which fell out between Cain and Abel illustrated
the hatred that subsists between the two cities, that of
God and that of men. The wicked war with the wicked; the good also war with the wicked.

Augustine *The City of God*

As I prepared for this lesson something occurred to me—my
children have grown up in a country that has been at constant war.
They don't know what peace is. My thirteen- and eight-year old children have never known a time that the United States wasn't fighting
someone. Necessary though it may be, it saddens me.

I know many good folks who've worn the uniform of our armed
services, and I appreciate their service. Were it not for the success
God gives soldiers, where might we be as a nation? Soldiers and warfare speak to a reality that is telling about human nature, and that is
that our sinful, fallen states demand a measure of earthly justice. This
justice points to the higher truth that there must be some standard

by which we determine justice itself. God is present in this definition for the Christian. Therefore, we look not for perfect justice from our God, but for complete mercy. His mercy is afforded through Christ our Lord.

Yet, justice will continue to be given in earthly terms. Those terms are sometimes as small as fines and as large as capital punishment. Warfare is a country's attempt at justice in many cases. In other examples, war exists because of greed and the feeling that a nation must strive for more and to be better. If a nation were to act as Christ would have us act, it would be perceived as weakness. To open our borders and share our goods would expose us to abuse and misuse. Therefore, we must be selective as a nation with whom we aid.

Laws exist because they are necessary. They are necessary because humanity is sinful. As I began to reflect on war from a biblical point of view, it led me to highlight "the way of Cain" as it was called later on.

DEFINING "THE WAY OF CAIN"

The "way of Cain" is mentioned in Jude 11 when Cain was used as the prime example associated with murder. Cain was, after all, the first to murder. In Jude, the way of Cain was spiritual murder through false teachings. Literally, the way of Cain is the way of death—of killing or murder. This way is unloving towards others with Christ's love (1 John 3:11–12) and displays the struggle of fallen humanity with our base desires (cf. Genesis 4:7). Accompanying the way of Cain is a weak faith in God's plan as evidenced by Cain not offering his sacrifice to God in faith as his brother Abel did (Hebrews 11:4).

Josephus informs us that the building of the city of Enoch by Cain (Genesis 4:16–17) demonstrated his proclivity toward tyrannizing his neighbors. The boundaries that Cain established for his city led him to resort to violence, and by this he lived through cunning and deceit. Josephus wrote that Cain's descendants became "intolerable in war, and vehement in robberies; and if anyone were slow to murder people, yet was he bold in his profligate behavior, in acting unjustly and doing injuries for gain" (*Antiquities* 1.2.2). To those who lived during Josephus' time and after, following the way of Cain was something commented on in the church. Even the preeminent bishop Augustine, as noted above, viewed the way of Cain in conjunction with the city of man versus the city of God, which was represented by the church.

GOD & WARFARE IN ISRAEL

When God knew that Israel would demand a king, one of his stipulations for the godly king was that he not acquire many horses or require the Israelites to return to Egypt for such purposes (Deuteronomy 17:16). Egypt was an exporter of horses for centuries. Samuel even foretold when Israel asked for a king that he would make citizens horsemen in warfare (1 Samuel 8:11)—something we refer to as "conscription." Even King David kept some horsemen when he would conquer other kingdoms (2 Samuel 8:4). Solomon, however, amassed forty thousand stalls for his horses (1 Kings 4:26; 10:26–28).

> Woe to those who go down to Egypt for help and rely on horses, who trust in chariots because they are many and in horsemen because they are very strong, but do not look to the Holy One of Israel or consult the Lord! And yet he is wise and brings disaster; he does not call back his words, but will arise against the house of the evildoers and against the helpers of those who work iniquity. The Egyptians are man, and not God, and their horses are flesh, and not spirit.

When the Lord stretches out his hand, the helper will stumble, and he who is helped will fall, and they will all perish together. (Isaiah 31:1–3)

How then can you repulse a single captain among the least of my master's servants, when you trust in Egypt for chariots and for horsemen? Moreover, is it without the Lord that I have come up against this land to destroy it? The Lord said to me, Go up against this land and destroy it. (Isaiah 36:9–10)

The way of Cain trusts in instruments of warfare. However, God's people were to trust in Him. Recall the account of Gideon recorded in Judges. He began with many soldiers and wound up with only a few hundred. Why? Because God wanted His people to know it was Him who won their battle, and not the sophistication of the military industrial complex.

THE PRINCE OF PEACE'S WAY

Isaiah 2 was understood by the church as Messianic in its tone. The last days of verse 1 were cited in the New Testament as the time of Christ (cf. Acts 2:17; Hebrews 1:2; 1 Peter 1:5, 20). Jesus as the Prince of Peace (Isaiah 9:6–7; compare with Luke 2:14) would bring a way of peace that no longer sought warfare. He would urge, through Peter, that His disciples "seek peace" (1 Peter 3:11).

He shall judge between the nations, and shall decide disputes for many peoples; and they shall beat their swords into plowshares, and their spears into pruning hooks; nation shall not lift up sword against nation, neither shall they learn war anymore. (Isaiah 2:4)

Many have interpreted this passage to mean that there would be no more warfare, ever. But as long as sinful man occupies this earth, there will always be trouble. However, as Christians, we are a holy nation (cf. 1 Peter 2:9) that doesn't seek warfare. Rather, we desire to preach the message of reconciliation (2 Corinthians 5:17–20). Reconciling people to Christ will be the only way to rid a person's heart of the way of Cain—warfare and killing.

THE LESSONS

Some might be prone to understand me as teaching a form of pacifism. I'm actually not. What I'm advocating—that I believe God is urging through Christ—is not pacifism, but the voluntary laying down of arms. As Christians, we no longer as a collective people seek war. I realize that in church history those who carried the banner of Christ did just that, and the result was the bishop Augustine formulating the just-war theory. Thomas Aquinas, a scholastic monk, refined the theory to include three criteria: the war had to be waged by a legitimate authority, there was to be a just cause, and those fighting must have the correct intentions. This theory, which originated in Christian theology, was created as the church and state became inseparable.

History aside, I don't believe that the Bible teaches that Christians cannot participate in the realms of authority that might use deadly force, or fight in wars. For example, the governing authorities are instituted by God, of God, and are His ministers (Romans 13:1–4). Soldiers came to John the Baptist, and he didn't tell them that they must quit being soldiers. Soldiers were converted to Christ. Think of Cornelius the Roman centurion. He wasn't told to cease being a soldier. Paul wrote about, at the end of Philippians, the conversion of some of those of the household of Caesar. These are examples of Christians being Christian while serving governing authorities—authorities usually associated with pagan practices, mind you.

I also believe that an individual has the right to protect his or her life. This principle is apparent from the Law of Moses (Exodus 22:2). Some will want to enter into a discussion about Christians not being bound by the Old Testament. While that discussion is for another time, we mustn't neglect that "whatever was written in former days was written for our instruction" (Romans 15:4). How we regard the Old Testament, I believe, is not how the first-century Christians (who had no New Testament) regarded it. Please note how often it's quoted in the New Testament.

Moreover, Christ urged His disciples to purchase swords (Luke 22:36). Wayne Jackson believes this was figurative since the two swords weren't enough for all of the apostles.[1] I respect his scholarship and knowledge of the text, but I admit that I've always seen this passage as one that urged a measure of self-defense. This could have been to avoid a mass arrest of Christ's followers at the moment. Whatever the case may be, I must say that I see it more as self-defense, but not Christ's defense. Later in that same chapter, Peter lopped off a temple guard's ear and Jesus urged him to put away the sword (Luke 22:50–51). Jesus also used the imagery of a strong man protecting his goods without a rebuke for the action of the strong man when He explained the kingdom of God being upon them (Luke 11:21–22). Jesus used a similar illustration when speaking about the master protecting his house from the thief (Matthew 24:43).

FILL IN THE BLANK

1. The way of Cain is associated with _____.

2. When Israel had a king, God didn't want the king acquiring many _____.

3. Horses were exported from _____.

4. Jesus as the Prince of Peace would bring a way that no longer sought _____.

5. The Christian nation doesn't seek warfare, but participates in the ministry of _____.

DISCUSSION QUESTIONS

1. Many Christians understand this topic of militarism, self-defense, and war differently. What should a Christian do if he is required to participate in war, yet is a conscientious objector?

2. Since Christianity is not to be a militant people, does that mean that Christians should be passive?

3. What's the fine line, if any, between aggression and self-defense?

4. Should the United States still follow the just-war theory? Do they currently adhere to such a principle?

NOTES

1. Wayne Jackson, *A New Testament Commentary* (Stockton: Christian Courier Publications, 2012), 133.

6

COMPLACENT WOMEN

Although my fathers were nothing, poor, unlearned,
High God may grant me, I hope, a noble state,
Because my life is virtuous, by his grace.

Geoffrey Chaucer, "The Wife of Bath"

You can tell a lot about a nation by the conduct of their women. That may sound like an enormous burden to lay upon women as a sex, but I prefer to see it, rather, as a compliment. I remember once reading an etiquette book in which the author stated that in social situations, youths looked to adults as to how they should conduct themselves. Adults looked to the elderly in social situations, but in the absence of the elderly, men typically looked to women.

Women, in the Bible, have a prominent place in the view of men. In the book of Genesis, three particular occasions appear wherein the mystique of women is highlighted. In Genesis 2 when God created Eve, the first thing Adam did was to speak of her in poetry—

This at last is bone of my bones and flesh of my flesh;
she shall be called Woman, because she was taken out
of Man. (Genesis 2:23)

In Hebrew, the terms for woman and man are used as a play on words. Adam said, "She shall be called *ishah* because she was taken from *ish*." While these two terms are similar, they denote something entirely different. Therefore, from the beginning, a woman has inspired the poetic side of man. Think of the work of Homer, the *Iliad*. The entire work, which in Greek is a poem, revolves around the Trojan War, which was fought because the Trojan prince Paris abducted Helen the wife of Menelaus and took her for his own. Homer's entire poetic work revolved around a woman.

Later in Genesis, when the matriarch Sarah died, Isaac was grief-stricken. Abraham sent one of his servants to procure a wife for Isaac. When he brought Rebekah back, we read that "Isaac was comforted after his mother's death" (Genesis 24:67). A woman has not only inspired the poetic side of man, but she's also been a source of comfort during man's despair.

Jacob had worked for seven years to marry Rachel only to learn that he'd been duped—the heel-grabber had his own heel grabbed—and had actually wed Leah. The decision to work an extra seven years for Rachel was nothing to Jacob. We read that those seven years "seemed to him but a few days because of the love he had for her" (Genesis 29:20). In addition to inspiring the poetic side of man and comforting him in his despair, a woman has made the unbearable much more tolerable for man.

A good woman may be hard to find for one man, but when a nation lacks virtuous women, we see the deterioration of the people as a whole. The hand that rocks the cradle truly rules the world. I know many a man who has been made better by a good woman—

grandmother, mother, wife, or daughter. It's my hope that Christian women everywhere would realize the influence that they yield in the greater scheme of society.

WOMEN OF LUXURY

In Isaiah 3:16–24 we're reminded of God's desire for the Christian woman in regards to her appearance. Her character isn't to be judged by her adornment, but by who she is as God's daughter.

> Likewise also that women should adorn themselves in respectable apparel, with modesty and self-control, not with braided hair and gold or pearls or costly attire, but with what is proper for women who profess godliness—with good works. (1 Timothy 2:9–10)

> Do not let your adorning be external—the braiding of hair and the putting on of gold jewelry, or the clothing you wear—but let your adorning be the hidden person of the heart with the imperishable beauty of a gentle and quiet spirit, which in God's sight is very precious. (1 Peter 3:3–4)

A person may put lipstick on a pig, but it's still a pig. A beautifully adorned woman, without the right character, is as vile as it gets. You can't cover up an ugly character. The Judean women had so concerned themselves with their appearance that their character lacked. The attention they paid to their hair would come back to haunt them. God would see to it that they ended up bald (Isaiah 3:17, 24). Shaving a person's head exposed them to ridicule (Isaiah 7:20) and represented a mournful state (Isaiah 15:2; cf. 3:26)—something the Jewish women would experience.

As the father of a teenage daughter, I get how important looks can be. No one would argue that it's bad to take pride in one's appearance. That's not at all what I'm trying to say. What I want to convey is that a woman can be as beautiful as they come, but her character can make her ugly. As Christians, we should not allow the women we love to think that their worth is directly tied to their appearance. Chasing the fountain of youth is something most do, but there ought to be more to a person than their looks.

HOW LUXURY BREEDS APATHY

The luxury of Israel's women led them to believe that the power of their own hands bred ease when in reality it bred a condition punishable by the Holy God of Heaven. Had the Law of Moses had a place in their hearts, they would have known God's warning to the nation hundreds of years ago.

> Take care lest you forget the LORD your God by not keeping his commandments and his rules and his statutes, which I command you today....Beware lest you say in your heart, 'My power and the might of my hand have gotten me this wealth.' You shall remember the LORD your God, for it is he who gives you power to get wealth, that he may confirm his covenant that he swore to your fathers, as it is this day. (Deuteronomy 8:11, 17–18)

Their ease led them to complacency (Isaiah 32:9–13; cf. Amos 4:1–3). Their attitude was directly portrayed as the mindset of wicked Babylon (Isaiah 47:7–8).

Apathy, I fear, is an epidemic in the American church. A preacher I know was about to leave the country for a three-year commitment in the mission field in Africa. I told him how much I admired what he was doing, but added that I couldn't do it. It isn't the distance, time, or place that I couldn't handle. I couldn't cope with going to this foreign land and spending three years with people whose hearts are on fire for Jesus only to return to the apathetic American church. It would be so discouraging. I was telling a class this story, and afterward a sister told me about someone she knew who went on a two-week mission trip overseas who had the same feelings once he returned. The church would announce a need only to see nearly every head bow as if the members didn't want to be asked to do the service for the work of the local church. What a shame!

WOMEN OF DESOLATION

By the time that God destroyed the city, these luxury- loving women would have no men around. Therefore, they'd disgrace themselves to gain a legal and social identity (Isaiah 4:1). Their reproach would likely be what women often suffered after their land was conquered—rape. The term in the ESV given as "reproach" occurs in the context of rape (Genesis 34:13–14; 2 Samuel 13:12–13).

After the war, the ratio of women to men would be greater than before because the men of Zion would be murdered. In the ancient East, women were under the care of men during their lives—fathers, husbands, and then sons. With these lost through death, or in some cases divorce, the women were desolate. Only men owned land—the virtuous woman notwithstanding (Proverbs 31:16)—so a woman with no man to care for her had no form of sustenance. This state is treated at length in the book of Ruth. The remarkable tenet of Boaz's character was his letting Ruth glean from his field as an act of mercy and charity. Once Jerusalem was redeemed, the "filth of the daughters of Zion" would be washed away (Isaiah 4:4).

THE LESSONS

Isaiah did not explicitly lay the blame at the feet of the daughters of Zion. While at least some of them did share a portion of the blame, we have seen that they certainly are not solely to blame for Israel's destruction.

The biggest lessons that I see here applies to everyone, not just women. Being a superficial believer in Christ whose chief concern is outward beauty and appearance may in fact lack substance. I know several Christians who enter their daughters in beauty pageants as toddlers or even youths. I also know a couple of good Christian women who participated in beauty competitions as young adults. This isn't something I would have chosen for myself or my daughter, but I don't wish to judge them for it. Those sisters can participate in pageants yet resist the temptation to be ungodly women.

I do wish, however, that such things didn't exist. Not all are able to handle them with stride, and I just don't believe that I'd care to parade around to be judged as an object and not a person. Even the heathen Queen Vashti in the book of Esther refused to trot before her husband and his guests. I don't believe it pleases God personally, so I wouldn't do it. "Charm is deceitful, and beauty is vain, but a woman who fears the LORD is to be praised" (Proverbs 31:30). There are other things more worthy of pursuit than fading beauty.

There's a passage from Amos (6:1) where God pronounces a woe upon Israel, "Woe to those who are at ease in Zion," He said through the prophet. We in American have it made; our biggest worries are usually high-class, first-world concerns. Others are content with little to nothing and are on fire for God, while many of us are guilty of allowing our level of comfort in this world to be our premier pursuit. Spiritually speaking, our comfort level hinders a lot of the good we could do for Christ. I once read that life begins at the end of your comfort zone. How true! Let's not allow the pleasantries of this life to hinder heartfelt service to God.

FILL IN THE BLANK

1. You can't cover up an ugly _____.

2. Their ease led to _____.

3. The daughters of Zion's reproach was likely an indication of _____.

4. The biblical book of _____ portrays the desolation of women.

5. The heathen queen _____ didn't parade herself before her husband and his companions.

DISCUSSION QUESTIONS

1. Should Christians partake in beauty pageants? Why or why not?

2. If some participate in beauty pageants, how should those who disagree respond (if at all)?

3. How can the church fix its apathy problem?

4. If we live in relative ease, is it an indication of a diluted Christian faith?

7

THE FAITHFUL FEW

How I long for my husband—alive in memory, always,
that great man whose fame resounds through Hellas
right to the depths of Argos!

Homer *Odyssey*

Whenever I think of faithfulness, I always picture Penelope of Homer's epic poem, *The Odyssey*. The Trojan War had ended, but Odysseus had not returned home, and his wife Penelope held out hope that he was still alive though she didn't know for sure. Suitors occupied her house waiting for her to wed one of them, but she would not. It's a story of deep, abiding love. A story of fidelity. A story where you see just how great a wife's love is for her husband. I remember taking a quiz on the internet to determine which classical literary character I was most like. I had my wife take the same test, and the result was that she was like Penelope. She had no idea who Penelope was, so I assured her that it was a great thing given this faithful wife's character.

Amidst all of the infidelity of Israel, there were still some who had remained steadfast. You can always bet that God has His people somewhere. When all seems lost, there are some who haven't bowed the knee to Baal. The apostle Paul needed this reassurance when he was in Corinth. He had reasoned with the Jews and Greeks, but the Jews kept on rejecting him, so he shook out his garments and determined to go to the Gentiles from that point onward. Jesus appeared to him in a vision that night and assured him, "I have many in this city who are my people" (Acts 18:10).

There's only one story in all of Scripture that I can recall where God is not happy with the limited number of righteous people in a city. That city was Sodom. There were so few faithful people that God determined it was time to destroy the city because of the outcry against it.

GOD'S SENSE OF JUSTICE

The story of God's destruction of Sodom and Gomorrah teaches us that God doesn't take the judgment of a city and its people lightly. Nevertheless, when God comes to the point of destroying people, it is for persistent sin and with good reason. Before He informed Abraham of His plan, God pondered in His mind—

> Shall I hide from Abraham what I am about to do, seeing that Abraham shall surely become a great and mighty nation, and all the nations of the earth shall be blessed in him? For I have chosen him, that he may command his children and his household after him to keep the way of the LORD by doing righteousness and justice, so that the LORD may bring to Abraham what he has promised him. (Genesis 18:17–19)

God expected descendants of Abraham to keep His ways by doing righteousness and justice, and as spiritual children of Abraham, this is also the mantle that we Christians carry (cf. John 8:39; Galatians 3:7). The issue of God's judgment upon Sodom and Gomorrah was exactly because of their lack of righteousness and justice. Most people are content to label Sodom and Gomorrah as a city of homosexuality, and it was, but that wasn't all that the people were guilty of.

> Behold, this was the guilt of your sister Sodom: she and her daughters had pride, excess of food, and prosperous ease, but did not aid the poor and needy. They were haughty and did an abomination before me. So I removed them, when I saw it. (Ezekiel 16:49–50)

God determined to obliterate Sodom and Gomorrah because the outcry against them was great and their sin was grave (Genesis 18:20). Their sins were not only hedonistic, but they also impacted others very negatively.

Abraham pleaded with God that He spare the city if only so many righteous were found in it. The patriarch began with fifty and wound up settling with God on ten. There were not even ten righteous people in the city. Abraham's concern was that God would destroy the righteous with the wicked, thus making the justice of God unjust (Genesis 18:23). As it was, God was willing in His own righteousness and justice to spare the righteous and not allow them to be swept away with the wicked. Therefore, Lot and his family were given notice to avoid God's wrath, but obedience was required. When reading the fleeing of Lot and his family, we sense that they were hesitant to go. God wanted them to escape without looking back, but Mrs. Lot didn't obey God's command.

Thinking along these lines we see similar language used in Isaiah of God's own people. Judgement was coming to Jerusalem because they had behaved just as Sodom.

> For Jerusalem has stumbled, and Judah has fallen, because their speech and their deeds are against the LORD, defying his glorious presence. For the look on their faces bears witness against them; they proclaim their sin like Sodom; they do not hide it. Woe to them! For they have brought evil on themselves. (Isaiah 3:8–9)

Later on, the prophet declared that Judah was absent of the two things for which Abraham was to have been known—righteousness and justice (Isaiah 5:7).

THE RIGHTEOUS AMONG THE WICKED

Isaiah juxtaposed the destruction of Sodom and Gomorrah with that of Israel. For the former, the Lord devoted them to complete and utter destruction. For the latter, God would leave survivors (Isaiah 1:9; 6:13). As much was implied in the name of Isaiah's son, Shear-Jashub, which meant, "A remnant will return" (Isaiah 7:3). Those who would survive the impending assault of Jerusalem would be called holy because of their survival (Isaiah 4:2–3). Even when news reached Judah of a march on them by the Assyrians, God urged that they pray for the remnant (Isaiah 37:4). That remnant would "take root downward and bear fruit upward" (Isaiah 37:31–32)—some have read this passage as a reference to Christianity being spread from Jerusalem. God would not abandon the faithful though they were few.

You keep him in perfect peace whose mind is stayed on you, because he trusts in you. Trust in the LORD forever, for the LORD GOD is an everlasting rock. (Isaiah 26:3–4)

The idea of the remnant is discussed at greater length in Isaiah 10:20–27. Yet, it's interesting that it wouldn't only be those who survived the horror that was to come upon Jerusalem. He'd gather them from wherever they were (Isaiah 11:11).

THE LESSONS

I sincerely hope that we don't regard flippantly what should be treated as grave. The Bible lays down the narrative of what God did to His own people, and we sometimes forget that He sent them prophet after prophet after prophet. Does God have wrath? Absolutely. We mustn't neglect His longsuffering throughout the whole narrative. When you think about it, the kingdom took an idolatrous turn during the reign of Jeroboam in the tenth century B.C. Isaiah began his prophetic ministry in the eighth century B.C. Therefore, for close to two hundred years, God tolerated and tried to warn Israel to return to Him. Since none of us live that span of time, we can surely smile upon God's mercy in the opportunities and timetable that He gave Israel when we consider our own impatience with people who behave as Israel did.

God has His limits. I don't know if you've ever noticed or not, but God had promised Abraham to bring his offspring to the land of Canaan after they were servants in Egypt for 400 years (Genesis 15:13). Following that, God said, "For the iniquity of the Amorites is not yet complete" (Genesis 15:16). What a testament to God's patience! He gave the Amorites over four centuries to repent. It almost seems as if God was harsher to His own people than the heathen Amorites. I'd say that He only expected more of them since they had Moses' Law whereas such didn't even exist in Genesis.

I bring all of this up to encourage us to not speak so carelessly on a related issue. When Christians talk about war and the death penalty, it's a line of ideology. I know that the state has the right to punish the wrongdoer with capital punishment (Romans 13:4), but let's not forget that our own Lord was punished with capital punishment too. The state isn't always right in its execution of justice either in capital punishment or war. When I hear people make the comment, "We should bomb them!" I hear people treating the image of God with so little concern. Emotionally, we make those statements, but if we were the one to make the decision, I'd hope we did so with greater forethought. Moreover, I hope our statements about other nations, regardless of how depraved they are, doesn't show to God a contempt for human life—life that was created in His image that all of humanity bears and life that the Messiah suffered for in order to provide all humanity with the hope of salvation.

Faithfulness to God isn't measured by our worship. In Isaiah 1:11–16, Israel continued praying to and worshiping God. However, they had failed to live righteously. They lived idolatrous lives all the while "attending church." Have you ever noticed that sometimes some Christians live like hell throughout the week while living like Christians on Sunday? I had a Bible teacher tell me once years ago that one of her young students remarked, "My daddy's only a Christian on Sundays." This little girl couldn't have been but four or five years old, but she knew the difference. How sad it is that her own daddy set a poor example for her. She'll likely grow up thinking it's alright to worship right on Sunday and live like hell the rest of the week. I fear that preachers in the Lord's church have harped so strongly on worshiping God rightly that we've neglected to emphasize living the transformed life (Romans 12:1–2) while seeking things above (Colossians 3:1–5).

Finally, never underestimate the impact a few faithful can have. Had Sodom had only ten righteous people, God would have spared them. When I think about the United States—the land of the free and the home of the brave—I often wonder what's stayed God's hand from destroying us. Our blemishes have been one of slavery, abortion, same-sex marriage, and rampant sin. Could it be that God reserves His wrath on our country simply because of us faithful few who pray for our country and leaders? I've often wondered that. Thanks be to God that He would be so patient. If there's ever an incentive to pursue righteousness in this life, I'd suggest that this could be at least one.

FILL IN THE BLANK

1. God wanted Abraham to teach his household to keep the way of the Lord by doing _____ and _____.

2. List the other sins, in addition to homosexuality, that Sodom was guilty of committing: _____ _____

3. Isaiah's son's name (Shear-Jashub) meant, "_____ _____."

4. The remnant would take root _____ and bear fruit _____.

5. God keeps the person in perfect peace whose _____ is stayed on _____.

DISCUSSION QUESTIONS

1. How can you measure faithfulness, and how can you not measure faithfulness?

2. How might God's sense of justice be applied to His mercy and the gospel?

3. If God promised that a remnant might return, why would He have asked for them to be prayed for when Jerusalem was attacked?

4. Apart from divine revelation, how might we now discern God's acting in history?

5. Do we find ourselves as Christians neglecting to have compassion and respect for human life? How can we balance the proper respect for humanity with issues such as war and capital punishment?

8

HOPE APPEARS

If I find in myself a desire which no experience in this world can satisfy, the most probable explanation is that I was made for another world.

C. S. Lewis, *Mere Christianity*

This thought presented by C.S. Lewis is perhaps my most favorite of his. I've seen these sentiments shared by Plato, another author whom I admire—"A thing that desires desires something of which it is in need; otherwise, if it were not in need, it would not desire it. I can't tell you, Agathon, how strongly it strikes me that this is necessary" (*Symposium* 200b). The whole thrust of this statement appears in Lewis' chapter on hope. The very idea that we yearn for something points to the belief that there should be a parallel reality for our yearning. Put another way: if we have desires, there must be something to fill those desires. When we're hungry, food satisfies us. When we're thirsty, drink satisfies us. When we're lonely, companionship can fill the gap. However, when you and I find ourselves surrounded by possessions and company, seeing that all of our needs and most of our wants are met, and yet still have a void within, there must be something more. That something more is the reality of heaven, the place where we return to perfect fellowship with our Father.

As long as we all live on this earth, we'll want and will never be satisfied. We may learn contentment, but contentment is our adapting to what we have and not coveting more. The desires we have that nothing in this world satisfies points to the reality that we were meant for a relationship with God. Israel had squandered their relationship with God while not realizing that He had all that they ever could have needed and wanted. God's judgment would come upon them, but He would not leave them without hope.

Thus far in our study of Isaiah, we've seen all of Israel's problems. They had close to two hundred years or so of warnings from God through His prophets. Their downward spiral began when the kingdom split into two and the north began following pagan ways. This all accelerated when Ahab became king, and only degenerated further into apostasy from there. God's warnings and attempts at getting His people to repent indicate His patience and His love of His people. The time was coming for their judgment, but even though Israel would suffer, there would be hope for the future for those facing His wrath in the present. Israel's hope and consolation would come in the most unusual way—not a king riding on the white horse with the armies of God, but an infant born in a manger. That infant would be Israel's hope. Praise be to God!

GOD'S PLAN

The particular way that God chose to redeem humanity and His people would be in an unlikely manner. Even the apostles failed to understand that God's Messiah was not coming to establish an earthly kingdom as we tend to think of earthly kingdoms (Acts 1:6). The essence of His plan involved taking on flesh in the form of His Son.

Isaiah 7:14, in its context, referred not to Jesus but the son of Ahaz. However, for early Christians, the promises of the Old Testament carried a deeper meaning than its original context.

> Therefore the Lord himself will give you a sign. Behold, the virgin shall conceive and bear a son, and shall call his name Immanuel.

The name "Immanuel" means "God with us." It wasn't that Jesus was to have this name, but that the name given in Isaiah's prophecy communicated the truth that God would be with His people. The gospel according to John communicates this clearly as John emphasizes Jesus' deity. This is witnessed strongly when Thomas touches the Lord and proclaims, "My Lord and my God" (John 20:28). While the passage initially spoke about Ahaz's son, the gospel writers saw the significance of the passage as speaking of Jesus given the miraculous nature of His conception and birth through Mary, the virgin whom God chose to bear His Son—"But when the fullness of time had come, God sent forth his Son, born of woman, born under the law" (Galatians 4:4).

The Hebrew term translated as "virgin" is 'almah. It can be translated as "virgin," "maiden," "girl," or "damsel." It denotes an unmarried, pure young lady. However, when the Hebrew Old Testament was translated into Greek in the Intertestamental Period—the time period between Malachi and Matthew—the seventy Hebrew scholars who did the translating inserted the Greek term parthenos which meant expressly, "virgin." Many Jewish and contemporary academic Bible scholars refute that Isaiah 7:14 referred to Jesus at all because of the Hebrew term. What must be remembered is that when the Old

Testament was quoted in the New Testament, more often than not did the quotation derive from the Greek Old Testament (Septuagint, or LXX) rather than the Hebrew Old Testament. Therefore, the early Christians believed—as history informs us—that the Greek Old Testament was the Word of God.

Since the original meaning of the text took on a new meaning for the New Testament writers, how can we say that they didn't just proof-text passages that seemed to fit their narrative of the gospel? What we must remember is that Jesus, after His resurrection, explained to His disciples how the Scriptures spoke concerning Him (Luke 24:27, 44). The writers of the New Testament, when they *seem* to use Old Testament passages without regard to their original context, were given this interpretation from Jesus. See Christopher J. H. Wright's book, *Knowing Jesus Through the Old Testament*, for more on this topic of the Old Testament being used in the New Testament.

JESUS' LINEAGE

People today don't care as much about their lineage as perhaps older people and civilizations do and did. As Americans, we've nearly lost our ethnicity from our original homelands except through our surnames. However, to the people of antiquity, lineage was highly valuable and a matter of pride in many cases.

What we're first informed about the Messiah's lineage is that He would descend from Jesse, David's father (Isaiah 11:1, 10). He, like Jesse's son—Kind David—would be a king himself.

> For to us a child is born, to us a son is given; and the government shall be upon his shoulder, and his name shall be called Wonderful Counselor, Mighty God, Everlasting Father, Prince of Peace. Of the increase

of his government and of peace there will be no end, on the throne of David and over his kingdom, to establish it and to uphold it with justice and with righteousness from this time forth and forevermore. The zeal of the LORD of hosts will do this. (Isaiah 9:6–7)

The promise to give Jesus the throne of his father David reiterated the promise that God had made to David many years ago: "And your house and your kingdom shall be made sure forever before me. Your throne shall be established forever" (2 Samuel 7:16; cf. Genesis 49:10). This was how the early Christians understood the reign of Christ—as an inheritor of the throne of David (Acts 2:30–31; 7:49). Therefore, when we read the genealogy of Matthew tracing from Jesus to David to Abraham, Matthew was showing that Christ was indeed the legitimate heir of whom the prophets foretold.

GODS CONSORTING WITH WOMEN

Greco-Roman gods often consorted with women to produce offspring who were referred to as "heroes." Many people in antiquity saw the birth of Jesus as something similar, and scholars of comparative religions make the same claim in our own time. However, an early Christian named Justin Martyr (died c. AD 165) had the following to say on the matter—

But lest some, not understanding the prophecy now cited [Isaiah 7:14], should charge us with the very things we have been laying to the charge of the poets who say that Jupiter went in to women through lust, let us try to explain the words. This, then, "Behold, a virgin shall conceive," signifies that a virgin should conceive without intercourse. For if she had had intercourse with any one whatever, she was no longer a virgin; but the power of God having come upon the virgin, overshadowed her, and caused her while yet a virgin to conceive....not by intercourse, but by power. (*First Apology* 33)

I mention this only to show that many of the silly arguments used by folks then and now have already been answered by others.

THE LESSONS

God always has a plan. His plan always includes hope. Galatians 4:4 speaks beautifully to the eternal purpose of God in Christ Jesus. First, we see that God always shows up. He showed up when three Jewish boys were in a fiery furnace. He showed up for Daniel when he was facing a lion. He showed up when His people, the Jews, were looking down the barrel of Persian extinction in Esther. Therefore, God would show up for the sake of humanity. You and I can always be sure that God will show up on His time, not ours.

Second, when God shows up, don't be surprised if He uses another person. God chose Mary. When the time came for Him to arrive, He used this pious Jewess to bring forth His Son. When Jacob and his sons faced famine, God gave them Joseph to aid in the divine plan. When Israel was weighted down under the yoke of Egyptian bondage, God sent them Moses. When the Ethiopian Eunuch pondered a passage from Isaiah, God sent Philip to him. When Saul of Tarsus saw the light and was blinded, God sent him to Ananias. God often uses people in His plan, and Mary was the woman for the job here. We can all point to people who touched us in some special way. These people blessed us when we needed it most. God used them for us, so be sure that you let Him use you to be a blessing in another's life.

Finally, God always has it His way. He set up a system through Moses that was to lead the Jews to distinction among the Gentiles and to prepare the way for Christ. It was under this system that God would work to show up using Mary. This very system was used by His Son to point humanity to Himself. However, sometimes we have to try it our way. Abraham and Sarai tried it their way by having Abraham produce offspring with Hagar. Moses tried it his way by striking the rock when he was supposed to speak to it. Saul of Tarsus tried it his way and turned out to be persecuting the church of God. Each way failed and had consequences. So, will you try it your way, or will you do it God's way?

FILL IN THE BLANK

1. The name "Immanuel" means "_____ _____."

2. The term "virgin" in Isaiah 7:14 was placed there as such by the translators of the Greek Bible during the _____ Period. This is the period between _____ and _____.

3. Isaiah 7:14 originally spoke about a son of _____, but Jesus opened the understanding of His disciples to what the passage actually meant.

4. Jesus was to descend from Jesse, _____ father.

5. The lineage of Jesus' relationship to David is recorded in _____ gospel.

DISCUSSION QUESTIONS

1. Considering that Isaiah was written in the eighth century B.C., discuss how prophecies in the Old Testament validate the inspiration of the Bible.

2. It's clear that the New Testament authors understood the Old Testament differently from many Jewish interpretations during the first century that led to a rejection of Jesus. To what degree should we read the Old Testament as the early church did?

3. Since the early church understood the Old Testament a certain way, how closely should we follow church tradition in interpreting Scripture?

4. I gave two examples of how people try to refute that Isaiah spoke about Jesus (the term in Isaiah 7:14 and the gods consorting with women). How shall you respond when someone brings up what seems like a legitimate refutation against something the Bible says?

5. Choose one of the examples of how God used a person to bring hope to His people and discuss what we can learn about the nature of God from that example.

9

THE MISSION OF GOD'S HOPE

The soul that is altogether courageous and great is marked above all by two characteristics: one of these is indifference to outward circumstances; for such a person cherishes the conviction that nothing but moral goodness and propriety deserves to be either admired or wished for or striven after, and that he ought not to be subject to any man or passion or any accident or fortune. The second characteristic is that, when the soul is disciplined in the way above mentioned, one should do deeds not only great and in the highest degree useful, but extremely arduous and laborious and fraught with danger both to life and to many things that make life worth living.

Cicero *On Duties*

Very few of my age-group (the thirties) use the term "duty." We sometimes bemoan having to do anything, but people in antiquity were used to performing what was expected of them. In the foundational epic of Rome (*Aeneid*), which was written and produced during Augustus' reign, the central character Aeneas is noted for his duty, or what the Latins called *pietas*. The Roman sense of duty meant performing a task for whom one owed an obligation. Sound familiar? That's because it sounds very biblical too: "Pay to all what is owed to them: taxes to whom taxes are owed, revenue to whom revenue is owed, respect to whom respect is owed, honor to whom honor is owed" (Romans 13:7). Even the Old Testament carries this line of thinking: "Do not withhold good from those to whom it is due, when it is in your power to do it" (Proverbs 3:27).

While we seldom use the term duty, perhaps because we Americans are "free," it wouldn't hurt our society if it had a greater sense of duty rather than entitlement. Our grandparents and great-grandparents had this urging of duty when they went to war after Pearl Harbor was attacked by the Japanese. Even the Japanese had a belief of duty to their Emperor when they became kamikaze. The Japanese were so duty-bound to their Emperor that their lives were his to use as he wished, even in suicide. To the Japanese, that was an honorable death. Our American ancestors who fought back in response to them had a sense of duty to their families and our country. Sadly, since then people have not viewed themselves as serving of others. We've become more selfish.

When God sent His Messiah to earth, Christ's entire life was in service to God and for humanity. Even His forerunner, John the Baptist, was duty-bound not only to Christ but to the will of God as one of His prophets. If we as Christians viewed ourselves as duty-bound to others, we'd certainly live a life akin to Christ's. However, before the Messiah came, His way was to have been prepared.

PREPARING THE WAY

The salvation of Israel would appear as an infant who eventually grew into a man. Once the Messiah was at a particular point in His life, God would send a prophet, who we know was John the Baptist, to prepare His way. Isaiah foretold it—

> Comfort, comfort my people, says your God. Speak tenderly to Jerusalem, and cry to her that her warfare is ended, that her iniquity is pardoned, that she has received from the LORD's hand double for all her sins. A voice cries: "In the wilderness prepare the way of the LORD; make straight in the desert a highway for our God. Every valley shall be lifted up, and every mountain and hill be made low; the uneven ground shall become level, and the rough places a plain. And the glory of the LORD shall be revealed, and all flesh shall see it together, for the mouth of the LORD has spoken." (Isaiah 40:1–5)

In John 1:19–23, the religious leaders of Jesus' day went to John to examine him and determine who he was in God's plan. John confessed that he wasn't the Christ, so they asked if he were Elijah—a reference to Malachi 4:5. John wasn't Elijah per se, but Jesus identified him as a type of Elijah who appeared in fulfillment of the prophecy (Matthew 11:13–14; 17:10–13; Luke 1:17). John didn't lie to those present because those who inquired wanted to know if he was Elijah. The Jews believed that Elijah himself would return while the prophecies were not as literal as they took them to be. They also wondered if John wasn't "the Prophet"—a reference to Moses' words in Deuteronomy 18:15–18 (cf. John 7:40). John's response to their inquiring about his person was to quote Isaiah 40:3–5.

When we think of the religious leaders being so scrupulous and inquisitive, we may be prone to believe that they were sticks in the mud. However, what the Bible doesn't explicitly record for us that history does was that many Messianic-type figures arose claiming to be God's Messiah. For example, in Acts 5:36–37 two particular messianic figures were named—Theudas and Judas the Galilean. Josephus, in his *Antiquities*, informs us a little about these folks.

He wrote of Theudas that he was a magician who tried to accumulate a following while proclaiming that he was a prophet. A troop of horsemen were sent and slew him and his followers, thus proving that he was not, in fact, the Messiah (*Antiquities* 20.5.1). A similar fate befell Judas the Galilean (*Antiquities* 17.1.1, 2, 6); however, Judas' efforts lasted longer and were a bit more successful than Theudas' were. Jesus had promised that many would arise claiming to be Messiah (Mark 13:6), so the history of what took place before Jesus' ministry explains the religious leaders' skepticism of Him. Those leaders had already seen false messiahs, so their guard was up to reject the actual Messiah. Nevertheless, Isaiah's passage and John's usage of that passage were meant to point people to God's Messiah.

THE MESSIAH'S MINISTRY

There are many details recorded in the Bible that we tend to gloss over because we cannot see their significance. However, God inserted them for a purpose, and for the ancient audiences those details were relevant. What we first learn from Isaiah was that the Messiah would have God's Holy Spirit rest upon Him, "And the Spirit of the LORD shall rest upon him" (11:2). At Jesus' baptism, we witness the Holy Spirit descend as a dove to rest upon Christ (Matthew 3:16; Mark 1:10; Luke 3:22; 4:1).

One reason why Judas of Galilee might have had the success he did was that Isaiah hinted at a Galilean ministry. "In the former time he brought into contempt the land of Zebulun and the land of Naphtali, but in the latter time he has made glorious the way of the sea, the land beyond the Jordan, Galilee of the nations" (Isaiah 9:1–2). Jesus' ministry began in Galilee (Matthew 4:13–16). The Messiah's ministry consisted of judging the earth with righteousness. His righteous judgment saw to the needs of the poor and meek (Isaiah 11:4–5). We learn that Jesus had the authority to judge, "And he has given him authority to execute judgment, because he is the Son of Man" (John 5:27). His judgment and righteousness healed those who were brokenhearted (Isaiah 61:1–2). Jesus read from the scroll of Isaiah in the synagogue and proclaimed that it spoke of Him (Luke 4:18–19). Finally, even Gentiles would seek the Messiah (Isaiah 11:10; 60:3, 5), and such sought Jesus. The first we read of seeking Him were the Magi at His birth (Matthew 2:1–2). The Gentiles would trust in His name (Matthew 12:21; Luke 2:32), and even Greeks sought Him (John 12:20–21).

Jesus was chosen by God as the chief cornerstone (Isaiah 28:16). At one point, John the Baptist's disciples were sent by him to inquire of who Jesus was (Matthew 11:2–5). Jesus' told them that to give a reply to John that alluded to a passage from Isaiah that described His ministry—

> In that day the deaf shall hear the words of a book, and out of their gloom and darkness the eyes of the blind shall see. The meek shall obtain fresh joy in the LORD, and the poor among mankind shall exult in the Holy One of Israel. (Isaiah 29:18–19)

Jesus' judgment and righteousness made Him God's lawgiver of the New Testament (covenant) written about in Jeremiah 31:31–34.

Isaiah saw the Messiah as a Lawgiver (Isaiah 42:1–4), and Matthew attributed Isaiah's prophecy to Jesus Christ (12:18–20).

LESSONS

God had a will for John the Baptist's life, and God had a will for the life of His Messiah. When we submit our lives to God in obedience to the gospel, we commit our lives to the service of our Creator. Some of us will discover where God wants us and how He wants to use us. Sometimes, as in the story of Esther, it will be by doing the most we can to accomplish good to His glory just as Esther did wherever we may find ourselves. At other times, perhaps, it may be that like Nehemiah we have something weighing on our heart that should provoke us to action for God (Nehemiah 2:12; 7:5). Don't misunderstand me, I'm not saying that God manipulates us by operating in our hearts. Rather, when we have a zeal for God and His matters, could it not be said that the Lord put it in our hearts to do thus and such for Him?

If you notice, leading up to Nehemiah 2:12, things took place that demonstrate to us just how spiritually minded Nehemiah was. First, Nehemiah had a concern for things about God when he asked about the Jews and Jerusalem. If you don't care, you typically won't ask. Second, when he heard the discouraging report, he was moved to weeping and mourning. If you care enough to ask and get a report without being affected, you may not be spiritually minded enough. Even in Nehemiah's prayer in chapter one, he mentioned the Lord's commandments and the knowledge of sin. Then, he also recalled the historicity of that Law as it traced to Moses. Next, he quoted from that Law the promises that God had made to Israel. We see in chapter one the spiritual mindedness of Nehemiah. In chapter two, we see Nehemiah act in faith. All the while, Nehemiah continues in prayer.

As the events unfold, Nehemiah discovered that God's will for his life was that he rebuild the walls of Jerusalem.

To discover God's will for our lives, we need to be spiritually minded, know the Scriptures, and have a sense of duty towards Him. This sums up the lives of both John the Baptist and Christ. It should also define our lives. May we all adopt the mindset of the Apostle Paul: "But I do not account my life of any value nor as precious to myself, if only I may finish my course and the ministry that I received from the Lord Jesus, to testify to the gospel of the grace of God" (Acts 20:24).

FILL IN THE BLANK

1. The leaders in Jesus' day believed that the prophet _____ would come back himself.

2. Another person the Jews looked for was the _____ spoken of by Moses.

3. _____ and _____ of Galilee were thought to have been messiah's before Jesus.

4. _____ disciples went to ask Christ who He was.

5. Christ's response was to cite from Isaiah pertaining to His _____.

DISCUSSION QUESTIONS

1. What's the difference between having a mindset of duty versus entitlement?

2. Should someone have an official title or capacity for God to use them?

3. How can God, without divine revelation or supernatural intervention, communicate His will to people as to how He'd have him live their lives?

4. If a person doesn't feel as if they're living God's purpose for their life, does that mean that they are too fleshly minded rather than being spiritually minded? Why or why not?

5. There are some ways that every Christian is to serve God. What are some of those ways?

6. There are other ways in which an individual Christian may serve God that is not a way in which every Christian is expected to serve. What are some of these ways?

10

GOD'S SUFFERING SERVANT

He himself does not deny that he is the Son of his Father, that, heaven-sent, he has come to you at last, as promised, to help ailing mortals and to reconcile your people with his Father's long-standing anger, even as he wipes away the sins of your ancestors with his own virtues. I understand that your ancient scripture predicts his coming, that your forefathers foretold it, and his deeds prove it. And so, passing through the surrounding cities, he aroused the whole land with his great miracles, which no force or skill of man could perform....Do not oppose him in vain, but recognize him as your god.

Marco Girolamo Vida *Christiad*

As the narrative unfolded for God's people, they would not live to see the grandest of days. While I write this particular chapter, it's been just a few days since Paris was attacked by terrorists. On top of that, Syrian refugees are flooding other nations—America included.

There's so much talk about whether we should permit them entrance into our country, and all that goes along with taking in refugees, some of whom just might be terrorists. Facebook is a sad picture today. Yet, in the midst of all of this despair, there is hope to be found for the United States and refugees. For God's people and humanity, there would be hope to be found in Christ and His sufferings.

WHAT GOD'S MESSIAH WOULD ENDURE

Throughout Isaiah, and specifically in chapter 53, God's Messiah would endure more than He would inflict. Based on the last lesson, we read from the New Testament that Israel expected a particular type of savior—a political, military figure that would obliterate God's enemies with His armies. Yet, Isaiah gives us altogether a different picture than what the expectation was. This goes to show us that we must always be willing to yield our wills to God's will. Even when we may think we have it right, we mustn't be hard-hearted like the people of Jesus' day and insist that our "interpretation" is without flaws. Listen to reason, and be willing to be proven wrong: "The one who states his case first seems right, until the other comes and examines him" (Proverbs 18:17).

Above all, a defining mark of God's Messiah was that He'd be rejected (Isaiah 53:1, 3). Christ, doing God's works before the people's very eyes, was denied despite the signs He did in their presence (John 12:37–38). This rejection would eventually lead to His arrest and trial. While going before His accusers, He would submissively be led like a lamb is led to the slaughter, saying nothing (Isaiah 53:7). While Christ was before Herod's court, He didn't open His mouth (Luke 23:9). He would give His "back to those who strike, and [His] cheeks to those who pull out the beard; [He] hid not [His] face from disgrace and spitting" (Isaiah 50:6). While standing on trial, Christ

was spat upon, struck and slapped by those who heard Him pro-
claim that He would be seated at God's right hand and coming on the
clouds of heaven (Matthew 26:67). While He ministered, He pointed
to belief in who He was like God's elect as a part of providing salvation for those who were lost (John 3:16) so those who'd believe would
be the portion of the strong who'd be saved (Isaiah 53:12).

His suffering would be so that He'd be disfigured by it—

> As many were astonished at you— his appearance
> was so marred, beyond human semblance, and his
> form beyond that of the children of mankind—(Isa-
> iah 52:14)

When we read about the scourging of Jesus (Mark 15:15), what
escapes our attention was the horrible bludgeoning it was on the human body. Eusebius of Caesarea (ca. 260–339) was, behind Luke, the
first major historian of the church. He wrote his *Ecclesiastical History*
as a way to preserve the Christian life and also to show how Christianity had endured the pressure of false teaching and persecution. In
one portion of his historical writing, he recounted the horrible effect
scourging had—

> For they say that the bystanders were struck with
> amazement when they saw them lacerated with
> scourges even to the innermost veins and arteries, so
> that the hidden inward parts of the body, both their
> bowels and their members, were exposed to view.
> (*Eccl. Hist.* 4.15)

What the Bible records as Christ's scourging is lost to us. If you've ever seen Mel Gibson's movie *The Passion of the Christ*, you saw a pretty good portrayal of a Roman scourging.

Everything that God did through Christ's sufferings was for us. Jesus voluntarily took upon Himself our sin's guilt and punishment (Isaiah 53:4–5, 7–8), so when we read that "For our sake he made him be sin who knew no sin, so that in him we might become the righteousness of God" (2 Corinthians 5:21), we're reading what Isaiah foretold.

> He himself bore our sins in his body on the tree, that we might die to sin and live to righteousness. By his wounds you have been healed. (1 Peter 2:24)

What was meant for us would be something that Christ would take upon Himself—divine judgment. We couldn't do what He did, so He voluntarily became our substitute (Isaiah 53:6, 8). Our weaknesses prohibited us from accomplishing what Christ could (Romans 5:6, 8), and this highlights God's love for us. The shame of our guilt was further compounded, not in the voluntary sacrifice accepted, but in being numbered as a guilty man among guilty men (Isaiah 53:12). This is why we see our righteous, holy Jesus next to common criminals upon the cross (Luke 22:37). Once He'd died, the final courtesy of burying Him would rest with a rich man (Isaiah 53:9) who buried Jesus in his own tomb (Matthew 27:57–60).

The darkness would not last forever, though. God would not abandon the body of Christ to see corruption and decay (Acts 2:27)—something that King David wrote about so many centuries earlier. On the third day, Christ rose, and the tomb remains empty. You can go to Buddha's tomb, and his body is still there. You can go to Mohammad's tomb, and his body is still there. When you go to Christ's tomb, however, it's empty. The suffering servant of God would be exalted (Isaiah 52:13), and Jesus was in fact highly exalted by God (Philippians 2:9–10).

DID IT REALLY HAPPEN THAT WAY?

The late attorney Simon Greenleaf said, "Every document apparently ancient, coming from the proper repository or custody, and bearing on its face no evident marks of forgery, the law presumes to be genuine and devolves on the opposing party the burden of proving it to be otherwise." Others in antiquity attested to Jesus' death as a matter of historical fact.

> Now there was about this time Jesus, a wise man, if it be lawful to call him a man; for he was a doer of wonderful works, a teacher of such men as receive the truth with pleasure…He was Christ. And when Pilate…had condemned him to the cross, those that loved him at the first did not forsake him, for he appeared to them alive again the third day; as the divine prophets had foretold these and ten thousand other wonderful things concerning him. And the tribe of Christians, so named from him, are not extinct to this day.
>
> Josephus (AD 37–100)

> Nero…inflicted the most exquisite tortures on a class hated for their abominations, called Christians by the populace. Christus, from whom the name had its origin, suffered the extreme penalty during the reign of Tiberius at the hands of one of our procurators, Pontius Pilate.
>
> Tacitus (AD 55–120)

On the eve of Passover Yeshu was hanged.

Babylonian Talmud

Julius Africanus (ca. AD 160–240) quoted the historian Thallus in his *Chronography* as saying that Thallus recorded a cosmic event that included a violent earthquake (cf. Matthew 27:51) and great darkness (cf. Luke 23:44) in Judea during the Passover season of the year that Jesus died. Thallus wrote in the middle of the first century and seemed to refer to the events of Christ's crucifixion.

THE LESSONS

There's a famous saying, "It's always darkest before the light." Israel of old must have felt as if they were in their darkest hour when invaded by terrorists in their own days. The disciples must have felt as if they were in dark times when their Messiah was crucified. Hope for them was on the horizon. Jesus would rise.

Lately, I've adopted two lines of thought when I'm so bothered by life or worried about things falling apart. Recently, a fundraiser was being planned by an organization associated with the church, and the person in charge of all of the logistics was understandably stressed. This person put a lot of forethought into the event as well as making sure it went well. I told them, "Remember two things if you try your hardest and the whole thing falls apart: 1) God still loves you, and 2) you can still go to heaven." Those two thoughts remind me of what's important. I say them often to myself and to others.

A brother came into my study one day at church. He was extremely concerned because he'd been losing the battle in a struggle of his. He was given into temptation and sinning—privately, I might add. He was so bothered, and I asked him, "Do you think God still loves you?" He answered "yes." I said, "It's clear that you're bothered by your weakness, and you're hard on yourself. Perhaps you should be hard on yourself to do better for God. However, don't be harder on you than the prodigal's father was on him. That father, who represented our Heavenly Father, was more than glad to receive back His son."

We have to remind ourselves that no matter what happens in life, God still loves us, and we can still be with Him in heaven. You get scolded by your boss, okay. You failed that exam, alright. You totally have a bad day and curse like a sailor, there you have it. Among your worst day, God still loves you, and you can still be with Him in heaven.

FILL IN THE BLANK

1. A defining mark of God's Messiah was that He would be

   _____.

2. _____ of Caesarea recorded an account of a Roman _____ that helps us understand the disfiguration of Jesus.

3. God made Christ to be _____ who knew no _____ so that we could become the _____ of God.

4. _____ wrote centuries before that Christ's body wouldn't see decay and corruption, thus promising a short burial.

5. Two things to remember anytime life gets too hard are that: 1) God _____ you, and 2) you can still go to

   _____.

DISCUSSION QUESTIONS

1. Why was it necessary for God's Messiah to suffer instead of coming with God's armies to conquer the foe?

2. Does our modern emphasis on military and national defense miss the essence of Christianity? Why or why not?

3. When we spend efforts on defending certain truths about Christianity, are we trying to convince others, or ourselves?

4. Why do we often lose sight of what's truly important and allow worldly worries to overcome our joy in Christ?

11

CLEAN GARMENTS

Most manifestly also does Zechariah prophesy of Joshua, who was clothed with filthy garments (to wit, the flesh of a servant, even ours), and stripping him of his ill-favored raiment, adorns him with the clean and fair apparel, teaching us by the figurative illustration that truly in the baptism of Jesus all we, putting off our sins like some poor and patched garment, are clothed in the holy and most fair garment of regeneration.

Gregory of Nyssa *On the Baptism of Christ*

A rather common question that I'm asked is, "How should someone dress when going to church?" I believe that along the way different generations have tackled this issue. I recall a brother, some years ago, remarking to me how he wished that all of the men waiting on the Lord's Table would wear a coat and tie. Of course, when you and I go to certain places there is a manner of decorum expected. My grandmother and parents instilled in me that it was appropriate to wear a coat and tie to a funeral home to pay your respects to the deceased. Pretty old-fashioned, some might think. However, every Sunday I wear a suit and tie (bow-tie, of course) out of obligation that it's a gesture of respect.

In Exodus 19:10, Israel was to wash their garments before the Lord descended upon Mt. Sinai. When you think about the context, they had been traveling, likely stunk to high heaven, and water may not have been as plentiful. Yet, when they appeared before God, they were to have been consecrated with clean garments. The Bible doesn't say what kind of clothes, but that they were to be clean.

In the Bible, a metaphor is often used to communicate about our sinfulness or righteousness before God. The metaphor is often one's dress. I'd dare argue that while no one can claim Bible authority for how we should dress in worship, there is a manner of the appropriate dress before God that pertains to a person's soul.

STAINED CLOTHING

Earlier in our study of Isaiah, we spoke about the passage that portrayed Israel's sins as scarlet (1:18) and the meaning of that statement—that their sinfulness was habitual. When wool was dyed the color of scarlet, it was fixed. The statement here spoke to the permanency of sin because once wool was dyed this color it could not be removed. However, also in 1:18, God promised to make Israel's sins as white as snow and wool.

Wool was naturally white, so it was considered pure in that state. Throughout the Bible, white represents purity and cleanliness—"Purge me with hyssop, and I shall be clean; wash me, and I shall be whiter than snow" (Psalm 51:7). David's sin was such that he was stained and required cleansing—a cleansing only granted by God. The priest would dip hyssop in the blood of a sacrificed animal and then sprinkle it on the impure object or person to remove the impurity (Leviticus 14:4, 7; cf. Numbers 19:18–22). This cleansing that David sought, that God would give to Israel, reminds us of the cleansing that Christ gave the church:

> That he might sanctify her, having cleansed her by the washing of water with the word, so that he might present the church to himself in splendor, without spot or wrinkle or any such thing, that she might be holy and without blemish. (Ephesians 5:26–27)

The redemption of God, however, did not and does not come at no cost to the believer. Later in Isaiah 1:27, Zion would be redeemed by justice and those in her who repented by righteousness. Repentance was necessary.

Beware of a faith that doesn't cost you anything. This kind of faith can be called "cheap grace." We don't do what we do in order to have afterlife-fire-insurance. There's more to it than that. This offer of grace was rich. It cost God His Son, so don't think that it requires little to nothing of you. C. S. Lewis put this very well in *Mere Christianity*—

> Christ says 'Give me All. I don't want so much of your time and so much of your money and so much of your work: I want You...Hand over the whole natural self, all the desires which you think innocent as well as the ones you think wicked—the whole outfit. I will give you a new self instead. In fact, I will give you Myself: my own will shall become yours'....The process will be long and in parts very painful, but that is what we are in for. Nothing less. He meant what He said.

I hear Paul's words from Galatians 2:20 in that thought from Lewis. What the cost is to us pales in comparison to what it was to God. For Israel and us, the fullness of redemption came at the cross (cf. Hebrews 9:15). Yet, only through God acting first with grace do we even receive forgiveness.

ADD SOME BLEACH

God's acting to remove the stain of sin would present it as if the sin never existed in two ways, "I, I am he who blots out your transgressions for my own sake, and I will not remember your sins" (Isaiah 43:25). On the one hand, sin would be blotted out. This language has been described by some to have been scribal language. In antiquity when scribes would make an error in writing or copying, they were said to have "blotted out" the error so that it was as if it never existed (cf. Exodus 32:32–33; Revelation 3:5).

On the second hand, for our sake, God would not remember the sins once they had been forgiven. This isn't to suggest that God *can* forget because if He could He would not be all-knowing (cf. Psalm 147:5; Proverbs 15:3). Rather, He chooses not to remember, or hold against us, our former sins. "Love...keeps no records of wrongs" (1 Corinthians 13:4–5 NIV).

What's most astonishing is not just the fact that God forgives as He does, but that when He's made up His mind concerning a matter that He speaks of it as if it's already accomplished.

> I have blotted out your transgressions like a cloud and your sins like mist; return to me, for I have redeemed you. (Isaiah 44:22)

Before Israel actually repented and returned to God, He promised them that He had already blotted out their transgressions.

CLOTHED WITH SALVATION

Isaiah's metaphor of one's dress as either being sin or salvation is carried later into his prophecy when he wrote, "I will greatly rejoice in the LORD; my soul shall exult in my God, for he has clothed me with the garments of salvation; he has covered me with the robe of righteousness, as a bridegroom decks himself like a priest with a beautiful headdress, and as a bride adorns herself with her jewels" (Isaiah 61:10). Dress as a metaphor for one's spiritual condition continued throughout the Bible.

After returning from captivity, the rebuilding of the Temple ensued. However, due to the neighboring opposition, and apathy from Israel, the work was abandoned with only the altar having been finished and the foundation having been laid (Ezra 3:1–4:24). Sixteen years later, while the Temple site remained dormant, Haggai and Zechariah stirred up the people to rebuild the temple (Ezra 5:1–2). On top of that was the stigma that sin had displaced Israel. A defeated people returned to a defeated land, only to be discouraged from completing their task—that is, until messengers of God told them otherwise. Israel was mentally beaten. Could God really forgive them? Had He forgiven them? Would they be safe again in their old homeland? All these and more must have plagued their minds.

In Zechariah 3:1–5, Joshua the high priest is portrayed as improperly dressed. Israel's sins and self-righteousness had been like "polluted garments" (Isaiah 64:6)—a reference to stained menstrual clothes. There, Satan stood to accuse Joshua before the Lord. However, God forgave the sins of Israel, and He clothed Joshua with clean garments—the garments of salvation.

In a parable that Jesus told about the coming kingdom of God, he used the familiar scene of a wedding. One fellow came inappropriately dressed and was removed (Matthew 22:11–13). Those, later, who were victorious over their hour of trial wore white robes washed by the Lamb's blood (Revelation 7:13–14), and the church is clothed with the deeds of the saints (Revelation 19:8). We who are Christians are clothed with Christ, "For as many of you as were baptized into Christ have put on Christ" (Galatians 3:27). It matters that we're clothed with salvation. God has provided our dress.

THE LESSONS

We may often be misguided by what we wear to church on a Sunday. I've known Christians, and I'm sure you have too, that are so nicely put together on Sunday but their lives are a mess. People will try to hide behind what they wear as if their dress is the sole communicator of their spiritual life. On the other hand, I've known some sincere Christians who looked almost pitiful but whose character was godly. Don't think that you're fooling anyone by what you wear, because you're not. Most importantly, God sees through the façade of clothing and right into a person's heart, and it's His perspective that should concern us most.

Someone may well say, "Steven, we should always give our best to God." I'd agree with that to only a degree. What if my best is so much better than someone else's that it makes them feel inferior—at least as it pertains to dress—and serves as a stumbling block? If you'll recall, the passages in the New Testament about modesty were more about overdressing and being gaudy than about not wearing enough. I once made the "We-should-dress-our-best" comment to an aged preacher, and his reply was, "My best is my doctoral robes. Should I wear those every Sunday?" His point was taken. Notice:

Likewise also that women should adorn themselves in respectable apparel, with modesty and self-control, not with braided hair and gold or pearls or costly attire. (1 Timothy 2:9)

Do not let your adorning be external—the braiding of hair and the putting on of gold jewelry, or the clothing you wear—but let your adorning be the hidden person of the heart with the imperishable beauty of a gentle and quiet spirit, which in God's sight is very precious. (1 Peter 3:3–4)

Now I'm not saying that we should be flippant with our dress. Balance is needed in this discussion. Any one extreme—"Wear your best," or "God doesn't care how you're dressed"—is unlikely very fair. As far as physical clothing, we have direct instruction to dress modestly, but other than that, we need not be overly concerned with our physical clothing. I would hope that what concerns us most is our spiritual clothing more so than our physical dress.

FILL IN THE BLANK

1. Israel was only told to _____ their garments before appearing before the Lord in Exodus 19.

2. God's redemption comes at a _____ to everyone. Otherwise, it's _____ grace.

3. The language used in Isaiah of blotting out sins was _____ language.

4. Being clothed with garments of salvation is seen in Zechariah 3 when _____ the high priest is given clean garments.

5. _____ in the New Testament is the Christian's way of clothing themselves with Christ—the garment of salvation.

DISCUSSION QUESTIONS

1. Is there, or should there be, a dress code of sorts for worship attendance? Why or why not?

2. Is our modern concept of a dress code scriptural, or merely a convention of our own time and society? Is there such a thing as a "divine" dress code?

3. What other passages refer to paying more attention to the appearance of something while ignoring its substance? How was this looked upon by God?

4. When we think about faith in Christ "costing" us something, what in Scripture is identified as a cost to us? Consider passages such as Luke 12:51–53 and 14:26–27.

5. If Christianity may cost us something, what might be suggested by our faith when we live in relative comfort and ease?

12

A NEW NAME

Father Abraham, whom have you in Heaven? Any Episcopalians? 'No.' Any Presbyterians? 'No.' Have you any Independents or Seceders? 'No.' Have you any Methodists? "No, no, no!' Whom have you there? 'We don't know those names here. All who are here are Christians—believers in Christ—men who have overcome by the blood of the Lamb and the word of his testimony.' Oh, is this the case? Then God help us, God help us all, to forget party names, and to become Christians in deed and truth.

William Warren Sweet
The Story of Religion in America

I'm fairly sure that no man would like it if his wife were to bear another surname other than his own. What might God think when we wear names that He hasn't given us? Once upon a time, I called myself a "Baptist," because that's what I thought I was. A brother asked me years ago, "Steven, what denomination are you?" I answered, "A Baptist." He said, "Nope." I said, "A Church of Christer." He said, "Wrong again. You are a Christian." Ever since then, the answer has come easy—I'm a Christian. Nothing more, nothing less.

CHANGING NAMES—AN INTRODUCTION

If you've ever paid attention to the Old Testament, there were often times when names of prominent characters were changed. What often escapes our twenty-first century, Western minds is that in the Ancient East, names were representative of a person's character. As the names were changed in the Old Testament, they were to reflect the individual's character as it then related to either God or an interaction with Him or promise made by Him. Please note the following examples:

1. "Abram" (Exalted Father) became "Abraham" (Father of a Multitude).
2. "Sarai" (Princess) became "Sarah" (Mother of Nations).
3. "Jacob" (Heel Grabber, or Deceiver) became "Israel" (He who strives with God).
4. "Simon" (God has heard) became "Peter" (Rock).
5. "Saul" (Asked For, or Inquired of God) became "Paul" (Little).

The Bible doesn't necessarily say why names were changed, but they often represented a new identity. The new character was meant to convey the person's relationship to God and His mission for their life, for better or worse. Remember that Naomi ("Pleasant") changed her name to "Mara"—which meant "bitter"—because of all that had befallen her. Even her sons' names were indicative of their state-of-health, but "Obed" (Servant) would become a restorer of her life and be a grandfather of David (Beloved). The name of our Lord, "Jesus", means "God Saves." Even the name listed earlier in Isaiah, "Immanuel", meant "God with us." These names communicated God's interaction with His people.

ISRAEL'S SHAME

Reflective in Israel's shame were the names they were to be called as a result of being dispossessed from the land that God gave to them. They would be called, "Forsaken" and their land "Desolate" (Isaiah 62:4). In the Ancient East, whenever people were conquered, it was sometimes said that their gods had been defeated by their conqueror's gods. At other times, it was said that people's gods abandoned them. God made it clear that it wasn't that He would have been defeated, but that He had left Israel and gave them into the hands of their foe.

After military campaigns, lands were not as luscious as they might have been before the war for obvious reasons. Since many kings conscripted their soldiers rather than pay them, one thing they permitted was for their soldiers to raid areas and keep whatever loot they obtained as payment for service. Armies then were rather a dangerous type in their methods of warfare, unlike what we might think of today regarding cruelty and excess. Women were raped, and if pregnant they were cut open, and children were dashed against whatever killed them (cf. Psalm 137:9; 2 Kings 8:12; Hosea 13:16; Nahum 3:10). The picture we gather when reading Isaiah is that they would have been conquered and carried off into exile. However, there was more to that. Israel would bear the shame of their name based on how they would have been conquered. They would be "Forsaken" and left "Desolate."

SHAME DOESN'T LAST FOREVER

God promised that their shame would not last forever. They would not be called for what they were, but by what God wanted them to be.

> The Gentiles shall see your righteousness, And all kings your glory. You shall be called by a new name, Which the mouth of the Lord will name. (Isaiah 62:2)

In the immediate context, Israel's name would be changed from "Forsaken" and "Desolate" to "My Delight is in Her" and "Married" (Isaiah 62:4). God had divorced Israel to send her away.

> Where is your mother's certificate of divorce, with which I sent her away? Or which of my creditors is it to whom I have sold you? Behold, for your iniquities you were sold, and for your transgressions your mother was sent away. (Isaiah 50:1; cf. Jeremiah 3:8)

However, when He permitted many exiles to return to the land, they would be God's wife—an illusion Jesus later used of the church (Ephesians 5:32). They would also receive other names indicative of their relationship with God.

> And they shall call them The Holy People, The Redeemed of the Lord; And you shall be called Sought Out, A City Not Forsaken. (Isaiah 62:12)

The implications of a new name accompanying a new identity

didn't end with the return from exile. It went on with the promises of the Messiah. Chapters 60–62 were a part of a continuous thought. In Isaiah 61:1–3, the Messiah was to be the bearer of good news, part of which included a new name.

THE NAME, "CHRISTIAN"

It would be in Antioch where the followers of Jesus would first be called "Christians" (Acts 11:26). God had said in Isaiah that He would call His servants by another name (Isaiah 65:15), and the name He chose was after His beloved Son. Gregory of Nyssa, a fourth-century bishop, wrote this on the name "Christian":

> Our good Master, Jesus Christ, bestowed on us a partnership in his revered name, so that we get our name from no other person connected with us, and if one happens to be rich and well-born or of lowly origin and poor, or if one has some distinction from his business or position, all such conditions are of no avail because the one authoritative name for those believing in him is that of Christian. (*On Perfection*)

The Latin suffix "ian" at the end of Christ's name means "from," "related to," or "like" when used as an adjective. When we say that we're Christians, we are saying that we're from Christ, that we're related to Christ, and that we're like Christ.

In Paul's letter to the Ephesians, he praised Christ "from whom the whole family in heaven and earth is named" (Ephesians 3:15). Peter even said that we may suffer as a Christian (1 Peter 4:16). To bear the name of "Christian" should not be a byword. It is a privilege. Are we living lives to glorify that name, or do we shame it?

THE LESSONS

The name that we're to bear is only that of our Lord, Jesus. We're not to wear any sectarian name that man has contrived. We're to be "Christians." There's no such thing as a "Church of Christer," or a "Church of Christ Christian." We're either Christ's, or we're nothing. We'd do well to remember that. The church is His, so it's the church of Christ. The church is His bride. The church is His body. At every turn, we see that the church belongs to Christ. Therefore, it should bear His name just as we should bear His name as Christians.

The shame that Israel carried through their names of reproach wouldn't last forever. Think about what sin people may know you by that you once were. Some might have been drunkards. Others might have been fornicators. Each of us could be called by our sins, but we're not. The shame of our sins that we once bore was removed at the cross. If people want to still identify you and me by our pasts, then that's on them. God, however, does not. I'm not my past, and you're not yours. We are Christ's.

One of my pet peeves is when some Christians insistently refer to all Christians as a "bunch of poor, miserable sinners." Granted, we are—though Christians—people who sin (cf. James 4:8). However, Jesus didn't die, I don't believe, so that we could be a bunch of poor, miserable sinners.

Paul said he was blameless regarding the righteousness of the law (Philippians 3:6), but he also acknowledged that he coveted (Romans 7:7–8). Was Paul a sinner? He had said that he was the chief sinner (1 Timothy 1:15), but he said that reflecting upon his life as a blasphemer and persecutor of the church. Jesus died so that we could become something more. When a person says that they're a sinner, I tend to take that in the same way that a doctor practices medicine and a lawyer practices law. Therefore, a sinner practices sin. Yet, John informs us that habitual sinners are lawless (1 John 3:4), but those who walk in the light as Christ is in the light continually receives cleansing from their sins (1 John 1:7).

As Christians, we are no longer our old selves, but a new creation—

> Therefore, if anyone is in Christ, he is a new creation; old things have passed away; behold, all things have become new. (2 Corinthians 5:17 NKJV)

> For our sake he made him to be sin who knew no sin, so that in him we might become the righteousness of God. (2 Corinthians 5:21)

I get that referring to ourselves that way (as sinners) is an attempt at humility, but it's a rather defeatist mentality. Jesus came and died so that we could have the abundant life (John 10:10). We sometimes focus too much on the Jesus who died on the cross and not enough on the Jesus who conquered death and rose from the grave as the Victor. He overcame the world so that we might do it too. We will always struggle with temptation and sin, but by God's grace, we are washed in the blood of the Lamb and made what God wants us to be. By His obedience we are made righteous (Romans 5:19). We must remember that the eyes of the Lord are on the righteous (1 Peter 3:12). If we practice righteousness as Christ did, we are then made righteous through Him (1 John 3:7). Sinners used to be who we were, but we're a new creation—justified, sanctified, through Christ our Lord.

FILL IN THE BLANK

1. Changed names in the Bible often represented a new
    _____.

2. Israel wouldn't always be called what they were, but what
    God wanted them to _____.

3. The relationship between God and Israel would be akin to
    that of a _____ and _____. Just how
    Christ related to the church.

4. It was at _____ that the disciples were first called
    "Christians."

5. Paul praised Christ through whom the whole family on earth
    and in heaven was _____ (Ephesians 3:15).

DISCUSSION QUESTIONS

1. Choose a name that was changed in the Bible and discuss
    how the meanings of those names represented the changes
    in that person's life.

2. Does it really matter what a person calls themselves (reli-
    giously) as long as they are "Christians"? Why or why not?

3. Does the sign in front of a church building truly identify a
    group of people? If not, what does?

4. If terms don't matter, then would it matter how we define
    "baptism" (as immersion rather than pouring, or anointing)
    and other religious terms?

5. Discuss some terms misused in the broader spectrum of
    "Christendom"—such as *Pastor*.

13

THE CHURCH ACCORDING TO ISAIAH

The world is driven and tempest-tossed by sins. Therefore, God has given to it assemblies—we mean holy churches—in which survive doctrines of truth.

Theophilus *Theophilus to Autolycus*

God has created and ordained three particular institutions that should be considered by all to be blessed. First, God created the home. All the way back in Genesis 2–3, we see that the first society God created was between a husband and his wife. They had children, and their home was a place of commonality. Cicero, the ancient Roman statesman, said that the family was "the foundation of civil government, the nursery, as it were, of the state" (*On Duties* 1.54). He believed that a healthy home made for a strong government, which is the second institution God ordained. The breakdown of the home in our society today reflects in the degradation of our country's morals. More could be said on this, but I'll not chase that rabbit into Alice's Wonderland.

Even when governments are uncivil, unfair, and corrupt, they are still God's ordained (Romans 13:1ff). Even though God had rejected Saul as king and chosen David to be king, David refused to harm King Saul for the simple reason that Saul was still God's anointed. The third institution that God ordained was the church. It is to this particular organization that we now turn our attention to in Isaiah as the last lesson in this wonderfully prophetic book. Since Isaiah contains so much about the gospel in it, it's only necessary that the church isn't left out.

ISAIAH'S PROPHECY OF THE CHURCH

Isaiah wrote in terms that many have understood as referring to the restoration of Jerusalem. This may, in fact, be true and a necessary understanding. However, the original meaning of Isaiah's words has been shown to have meanings that extend beyond the immediacy of what he wrote. Here's the passage referring to the church in his prophecy:

The word that Isaiah the son of Amoz saw concerning Judah and Jerusalem. It shall come to pass in the latter days that the mountain of the house of the LORD shall be established as the highest of the mountains, and shall be lifted up above the hills; and all the nations shall flow to it, and many peoples shall come, and say: "Come, let us go up to the mountain of the LORD, to the house of the God of Jacob, that he may teach us his ways and that we may walk in his paths." For out of Zion shall go the law, and the word of the LORD from Jerusalem. He shall judge between the nations, and shall decide disputes for many peoples; and they shall beat their swords into plowshares, and their spears into pruning hooks; nation shall not lift up sword against nation, neither shall they learn war anymore. (Isaiah 2:1–4)

Isaiah 2:1–4 is the prophecy Isaiah gave us regarding the church. The language here is closely akin to that of Micah 4:1–3. Considering that Micah was only a little after the time of Isaiah makes his words reiterate those of Isaiah.

> It shall come to pass in the latter days that the mountain of the house of the LORD shall be established as the highest of the mountains, and it shall be lifted up above the hills; and peoples shall flow to it, and many nations shall come, and say: "Come, let us go up to the mountain of the LORD, to the house of the God of Jacob, that he may teach us his ways and that we may walk in his paths." For out of Zion shall go forth the law, and the word of the LORD from Jerusalem. He shall judge between many peoples, and shall decide for strong nations far away; and they shall beat their swords into plowshares, and their spears into pruning hooks; nation shall not lift up sword against nation, neither shall they learn war anymore. (Micah 4:1–3)

Now, let's move on to an explanation of how these passages speak about the church.

DISCERNING THE PROPHECY

In each of these prophecies—which are nearly verbatim—a few common characteristics stick out that are worthy of our notice: latter days, the Lord's house, the law arising out of Zion, and the nations flocking to it.

In the first sermon preached in the kingdom of God, the subject matter was first driven by the miraculous manifestation of speaking in tongues. As the crowd present at the Feast of Pentecost—fifty days after the Passover—heard the apostles speak in their respective dialects, some inquired while others jeered. To explain the speaking in tongues, Peter spoke up and cited Joel's prophecy regarding the last days. "And it shall come to pass in the last days, says God" (Acts 2:17). Peter was showing that they had arrived at those last days mentioned in Isaiah and Micah, as well as some of the other prophets. Later, other New Testament authors also confirmed this fact. The Hebrew writer, in explaining the dispensation of the kingdom of God, wrote that God had "in these last days spoken to us by His Son" (Hebrews 1:2). Peter also later wrote that Jesus, who was foreordained before the foundation of the world, was revealed "in these last times for you" (1 Peter 1:20; cf. James 5:3).

While Isaiah looked ahead to the latter days, the New Testament authors wrote that they were living in those last days as the fulfillment of God's prophetic promises. Therefore, Christians are those "upon whom the ends of the ages have come" (1 Corinthians 10:11). The phrase "last days," or "latter days," is often mistakenly interpreted as the end of time when the judgment comes. The phrase was often used in the Bible to denote the end of an era, or trial, or some other time period. This was the way it was employed in Isaiah and understood by the church. "Days" was no more literal than when John said, "It is the last hour" (1 John 2:18).

In the New Testament, the church was often referred to as God's household. Paul wrote his first letter to Timothy so that he would know how to conduct himself in the household of God (1 Timothy 3:15). Gentiles were added to God's family, and the whole structure is being built into the holy temple of God where His Spirit dwells (Ephesians 2:19–22; cf. 1 Peter 2:5). Since the church is God's household, we are a family (Ephesians 3:15; cf. Galatians 6:10; 1 John 3:1).

We read that several nations came to Pentecost when the church was inaugurated (Acts 2:9–11). It was from there that the gospel went out. However, even when a considerable debate arose about Gentiles receiving circumcision, Paul and Barnabas went with others to bring the matter to the apostles and elders in Jerusalem (Acts 15). When Paul wrote his first letter to the Thessalonians, he noted how they became imitators of the churches in Judea (2:14). Nations had initially flocked to Jerusalem (Zion) though they were Jewish. Later, even the Gentiles came to Zion by imitation of the precepts taught from there.

> But you have come to Mount Zion and to the city of the living God, the heavenly Jerusalem, and to innumerable angels in festal gathering, and to the assembly of the firstborn who are enrolled in heaven, and to God, the judge of all, and to the spirits of the righteous made perfect, and to Jesus, the mediator of a new covenant, and to the sprinkled blood that speaks a better word than the blood of Abel. (Hebrews 12:22–24)

From these facts later taken up by New Testament authors, it's easy to see how Isaiah spoke of the church.

LESSONS

Have you ever had anyone say to you, "You can be a Christian and not be a member of a church," before? I think most of us have. Some of us may have even said it before at one time or another. However, it's a statement not based on fact.

In Acts 9:26–28, shortly after Paul was baptized and became a

Christian, he wanted to join the disciples. What led him to believe that he—as a new Christian (cf. Acts 9:17–18)—should or could join others who believed as he did? Sports fans assemble at stadiums and arenas when the game of their liking is being played. Golfers may find it necessary to join a country club that has a golf course and other amenities. Outdoorsmen are likely to be found congregating with others of like interest if they're not otherwise at an expo or Bass Pro. Logic would dictate that we might want to be with others who share our interest (i.e., book clubs, political affiliations, and social organizations).

Church membership is heavenly citizenship. To the Philippian Christians, Paul wrote, "But our citizenship is in heaven, and from it we await a Savior, the Lord Jesus Christ" (Philippians 3:20); "… so Christ, having been offered once to bear the sins of many, will appear a second time, not to deal with sin but to save those who are eagerly waiting for him" (Hebrews 9:28). Since our citizenship is where Christ resides, when he returns, He'll come to save those who are saved…those who are members—"Christ is the head of the church, his body, and is himself its Savior" (Ephesians 5:23). Since Christ is portrayed as the head of his body (the church), we must read Acts 4:12 through this lens: "And there is salvation in no one else, for there is no other name under heaven given among men by which we must be saved." Everett Ferguson puts it this way: "The church is the product of the saving purposes of God as expressed in Jesus Christ."[1] When Paul spoke of heavenly citizenship, he did so to a local church and not the church universal; although the truth is the same. When Paul preached the Gospel, he didn't simply make converts, but he planted local churches over whom he appointed and ordered the appointment of bishops/elders/pastors (Acts 14:23; Titus 1:5). We cannot be in "name" what we are not in "practice." Acts 2:42 is a theme of the entire book, and it included community, not individualism.

FILL IN THE BLANK

1. The three institutions that God ordained and blessed were: _____, _____, and _____.

2. Peter quoted from the prophet _____ in stating that they were in the last days.

3. The "latter days" don't always refer to the _____, but sometimes to the end of an era or period of time.

4. Since the church is God's _____, we are God's _____.

5. When Paul and Barnabas debated with others about circumcision, they took the matter to the _____ and the _____ at Jerusalem.

DISCUSSION QUESTIONS

1. What turns people off from joining the church?

2. Is church membership equivalent with salvation?

3. How should church attendance be understood when referred to as a salvation issue? Is it? Think about those unable to attend.

4. Discuss the purpose of God's church and what the Bible has to say about the church's purpose. The easiest answer is preaching the gospel to the lost, so if you speak about this one, ask what you personally are doing to that end, as well as

what your church does in your local community to that end. You'll likely find that there's more to be done.

NOTES

1. The Church of Christ: A Biblical Ecclesiology for Today (Grand Rapids: Wm. B. Eerdmans Publishing Company, 1996), 136.

APPENDIX: SATAN IN ISAIAH

> Cursed be [B]elial in his hostile design, and damned in his guilty dominion. Cursed be all the spirits of his [lo]t in their wicked design, and damned in their thoughts of unclean impurity. For they are the lot of darkness and their visitation is for eternal destruction. Amen, amen.
>
> 4QBerakhot[b] (*The Dead Sea Scrolls*)

An initial reading of Isaiah wouldn't yield an immediate notice of Satan—whose name means "adversary." However, what must be remembered is that, as has been stated before, the original contextual meanings of passages in the Old Testament were later used in the New Testament in ways speaking about the kingdom of God and items pertaining to it and certain people beyond the original meaning. A reading of the gospel accounts shows that the understanding of the Jews and early Christians towards sections of the Old Testament was to have seen the passages as representing a bigger truth. Matthew, for example, quoted Isaiah 7:14 as referring to Christ when the original context referred to someone else. Therefore, accepting a passage that had an original meaning as also having a secondary meaning isn't altogether wrong. Yet, the New Testament writers themselves do not state this interpretation of Isaiah pertaining to Satan that I propose.

Isaiah contains a foundational passage interpreted by some as representing the fall of Satan.

> How you are fallen from heaven, O Lucifer, son of the morning! How you are cut down to the ground, You who weakened the nations! For you have said in your heart: 'I will ascend into heaven, I will exalt my throne above the stars of God; I will also sit on the mount of the congregation On the farthest sides of the north; I will ascend above the heights of the clouds, I will be like the Most High.' Yet you shall be brought down to Sheol, To the lowest depths of the Pit. (Isaiah 14:12–15)

Initially, the passage was addressed as a proverb about the king of Babylon (Isaiah 14:4). However, certain descriptions were unfitting solely to him—such as having fallen from heaven. This description, when read against the backdrop of Daniel 2–5, explains the earthly ruler Belshazzar and how arrogant and prideful he was. Other readers saw in this passage the adversary, Satan.

In the Dead Sea Scrolls, Satan was referred to as either Belial, Prince of Darkness, or *Melkiresha'* (Heb. "My king is wickedness") according to *The Testament of Amram*. The Damascus Document linked Belial with Isaiah 24:17—"Terror and the pit and the snare are upon you, O inhabitant of the earth!"[1] Belial's activity here was his "three nets" as the document stated. It recorded that Belial set

forth before Israel three kinds of false righteousness which were for-
nication, riches, and profanation of the Temple.

Probably the earliest Christian interpretation of this passage as
speaking of Satan may be in Luke 10:18 which reads, "And he said
to them, 'I saw Satan fall like lightning from heaven.'" Now "Lucifer" literally means "day star." This could be what Luke meant when
he referred to Satan falling like lightning. The late New Testament
scholar I. Howard Marshall wrote, "It is hard to say precisely what
Jesus had in mind when He spoke of the fall of Satan [Luke 10:18],
but it is probable that the story of the fall of Lucifer (Isa. 14:12) pro-
vides imagery which Jesus used to depict the defeat of Satan."[2] The
earliest source that I could find connecting Luke 10:18 with Isaiah
14:12—besides what we might suggest of Luke's meaning—was from
Origen (died c. AD 251).

> Most evidently by these words is he shown to have
> fallen from heaven, who formerly was Lucifer, and
> who used to arise in the morning. For if, as some
> think, he was a nature of darkness, how is Lucifer said
> to have existed before? Or how could he arise in the
> morning, who had in himself nothing of the light?
> Nay, even the Saviour Himself teaches us, saying of
> the devil, "Behold, I see Satan fallen from heaven like
> lightening." (*On First Principles* 1.5)

Contemporary writers such as Tertullian (flourished c. AD 200)
and Cyprian of Carthage (died c. AD 258) also held to this position
about the passage from Isaiah.

What we might also consider is Isaiah's usage of Canaanite
mythical language. He noted how the Lord would punish Leviathan
(Isaiah 27:1) and how He cut Rahab into pieces (Isaiah 51:9). Both of

these creatures were Near East mythical monsters that Isaiah historicized. When we consider that the apostle Paul later noted that what pagans worshipped were in fact demons (1 Corinthians 10:20), the imagery that Isaiah gives us may refer to the demoniac in a Christian understanding. Therefore, Isaiah's passage interpreted as the fall of Satan may not be without foundation.

Whether we choose to hold to this interpretation or not is up to each individual. Our modern understanding of hermeneutics gives us great insight into the text, but we mustn't altogether discredit a hermeneutic that sees a meaning beyond the context. After all, this was how the New Testament writers interpreted the Old Testament—and that with opposition from the rabbinic interpretation that led the Jews to reject Jesus. I only ask that you consider the possibility.

NOTES

1. In Geza Vermes, trans., *The Complete Dead Sea Scrolls in English*, rev. ed. (London: Penguin Books, 2004), 132.

2. I. Howard Marshall, *Luke: Historian and Theologian* (Downers Grove: InterVarsity Press, 1979), 137.

PERSONAL NOTES

PERSONAL NOTES

PERSONAL NOTES

PERSONAL NOTES

PERSONAL NOTES

PERSONAL NOTES

PERSONAL NOTES

PERSONAL NOTES

PERSONAL NOTES

PERSONAL NOTES

PERSONAL NOTES

PERSONAL NOTES

PERSONAL NOTES

Made in the USA
Columbia, SC
25 November 2023

27104768R00070